INSTANT

AMERICAN
HISTORY

D0769720

INSTANT

AMERICAN

HISTORY

THROUGH THE CIVIL WAR AND RECONSTRUCTION

BY IRWIN UNGER, Ph.D.
WINNER OF THE PULITZER PRIZE

A Byron Preiss Book

FAWCETT COLUMBINE • NEW YORK

CONTENTS

LIST OF MAPS

INTRODUCTION

It's Friday night and you're in the mood for a *real* book. Your soul is crying out for a work of substance. You've always enjoyed American history, but lately that interest has chiefly been exercised in the area of Amy Fisher and The World War II channel on cable. So you head down to the local bookstore and scan the history section. What should you buy? To make sure you cover all the bases, you pick out an armload of titles on topics you dimly recall from an old college syllabus. Two months later the books remain where you left them, unread. The dust on the stack is pretty impressive. Time passes. A lot of time. You know it's all over when you buy a group biography about the cast of "Gilligan's Island." You feel cheap in the morning.

Now you can put aside those high-cholesterol tomes, and put the celebrity trash out with the garbage. It's time for *Instant American History*, a readable survey of American history from the early European settlements to the aftermath of the Civil War.

HOW THIS BOOK IS ORGANIZED

In each chapter, you'll get a list of the most important events in a period; a concise "who's who" of the principal players; and most important, tidy descriptions of the key events, people, and places that made America what it is today. These details are tied together with historical analysis and chapter summaries. Finally, a variety of light-hearted sidebars embellish the information you can actually use. You will come away enriched, with an overview of the trials of our great nation and enough anecdotes to let you star at the next cocktail party you attend where history miraculously becomes a topic of conversation.

AMERICA: THE EARLY YEARS

If you endured a high school or college survey course, you might remember the typical history book as a wasteland of names and dates, a monument to middle-aged male statesmen. You probably didn't find too many women or minorities in those pages, and the tone of the whole venture seemed oddly uncritical. The leaders tend to be self-assured and infallible, and the conquests (e.g. of Native Americans) and wars (e.g. against the Mexicans) seem just and necessary. Somebody always has to teach the heathen a lesson.

Alas, it's the happy duty of this book to throw a brick through the mirror of those illusions. *Instant American History* aims to tell you what *really* happened. Chapter by chapter, here are a few examples of the straight scoop you can expect to find:

CHAPTER 1: THE NEW WORLD

Columbus didn't discover America. Even if you define "discovery" in terms of European contact with the "New World," Columbus was preceded by the Norse from Scandinavia by half a millennium. Regardless of who came from Europe "first," the history books you grew up with usually neglected the perspective of the *original* inhabitants of North America. *Those* people didn't need discovery; they already knew where they were.

The motto of the Statue of Liberty ("Give me your tired your poor . . .") has emphasized the concept of America as a haven for the oppressed. But that's not the whole story. For example, many thousands of people were carried to the New World kicking and screaming— either kidnapped from England or sent across the ocean as their alternative to hanging. (Some chose the rope anyway.) And worst of all, thousands of Africans were forcibly torn from their homelands to live out their lives as slaves. Even religious refugees often had economic reasons for emigrating; their aspirations were material as well as spiritual. Many members of beleaguered religious minorities were no more broad-minded than their old world persecutors. To them, intolerance wasn't wrong in principle. The problem was that the wrong people were being persecuted.

CHAPTER 2: INDEPENDENCE

Few events in our nation's history have given rise to more myths than the American Revolution itself. Britain exploited and oppressed the Americans. Right? In fact, Britain was probably the best colonial power in the contemporary world, and under British rule the Americans prospered mightily. Americans were also the freest people in the world. Matters changed somewhat for the worse after 1763, but even then, for the thousands of American Tories—citizens loyal to the Crown—the Declaration of Independence was one long whine.

CHAPTER 3: THE CONSTITUTION AND THE PARTY SYSTEM

And then there was the formation of the Constitution and the beginnings of party politics in the young republic. You were taught that the Constitution was written by demigods. To use the vernacular, that's malarkey. The U.S. Constitution was made by a bunch of elitists. They were prosperous, educated, middle-aged white male landowners (did we leave anything out?) who had a healthy respect for the status quo. The document that emerged from their sweltering summer (no air conditioning! How did they do it?) in Philadelphia is considered brilliant today. But back then, the document almost wasn't ratified, and it has subsequently been amended twenty-six times.

How about the party system? The founders thought it represented everything wrong about government and plenty of Americans since then would agree. But people who agreed with one another about taxes, and banks, and religion joined together to fight those who disagreed and presto—Democratic-Republicans vs. Federalists.

CHAPTER 4: EXPANSION AND WAR

Here we deal with what Harry Truman called the dumbest war we ever fought. This was the War of 1812 against England, a conflict joined primarily because the British didn't like us trading with their enemy—France. New England opposed the war and tried to sit it out. Whatever could go wrong on the battlefield did, save for the glorious triumph of Andrew Jackson at New Orleans (which happened *after* an official peace had been concluded an ocean away, in Belgium).

CHAPTER 5: SEA TO SHINING SEA

Jackson, the hero of New Orleans, who made Americans feel good in 1815, would make many of them feel bad in the 1820s and 1830s when he entered politics. Jackson was a hard-bitten, opinionated, hot-blooded military man who leaped before he looked. On the day of his inauguration, the only way to remove the crowd of riffraff that jammed the White House was to open a keg of whiskey on the lawn outside. As president, Jackson deemed himself a man of the people, though he owned plenty of land and slaves. He dismantled the national bank because, he said, it was undemocratic. Actually, his hatred for banks (due to his own disastrous investments) probably had something to do with this move. In any case, Jackson did make principle out of his prejudices and in the process created the modern Democratic party. His opponents countered by gathering around the Whigs.

CHAPTER 6: MANIFEST DESTINY

Jackson and his party believed in "Manifest Destiny," the notion that Americans were entitled to do as they wished in that playground we call North America. Today this kind of thinking is called attitude. Canada and Mexico, not to mention Native Americans, Panamanians, Granadians, Nicaraguans, Cubans, still feel the effects of this doctrine. An early side consequence of the Monroe Doctrine was the Mexican War. After the cow chips had fallen where they would, the United States had gathered up more than a half million square miles of real estate in Texas, California, Oregon, and the Southwest. But after the feast comes the Alka-Seltzer, as historians say. That is, the immense expanse of new land, plus the diverging economics of North and South, would lead to deep political divisions, and eventually war. By the mid-1840s the South had become The Land of Cotton, the preserve of plantations, "poor white trash," and, of course, millions of black slaves. The North, on the other hand, had become a land of factories, mills, and towns, with an influx of Irish and German labor. Planters ruled in Dixie; merchants and bankers in the North. Slavery was prized in the South and despised in the North.

CHAPTER 7: A HOUSE DIVIDING

North and South argued about tariffs, railroads, and free land in the West. The biggest argument was over slavery and whether it should be allowed into the new territories acquired from Mexico in 1848. Thus began some of the most violent debates that ever graced the halls of Congress. Fisticuffs on the floor of the Senate were not unknown. To say there was ill temper on Capitol Hill would be like saying Vlad the Impaler liked shish kabob. How this political tension grew into war is a very complicated subject but all is clearly explained in chapters 7, 8, and 9.

CHAPTER 8: THE CIVIL WAR

The Civil War, as chapter 8 shows, was the great watershed of nineteenth-century American life. It was fought to preserve the Union, and one of its consequences was the destruction of slavery. Not out of idealism, however. Rather, Northerners saw that emancipating the South's slaves would undermine the Confederacy. Also, freeing the slaves made them eligible for the Union army and could hasten victory for the North. In those days, you could even buy your way out of the draft. The War of Brothers was a savage conflict in which more Americans died than in any other armed conflict in our history, perhaps more than all of them put together.

CHAPTER 9: RECONSTRUCTION

In 1865, the South was a wreck. Physical damage was everywhere. Worse, Dixie's slave labor system was gone.

And the region was out of political sync with the rest of the country. What to do about each of these were the major challenges of Reconstruction. In the end, Americans botched the job. The railroads, fences, and factories were rebuilt soon enough. But the former slaves were relegated—after a struggle—to powerlessness, poverty, and peonage. And after much blustering and "bloody-shirt" waving by the South's radical Republicans, Northerners proved to be wimps. In the end, the South returned to the Union on its own terms, without paying too much of a penalty for imposing four years of bloody war on the nation. In the end, there had to be a second "Reconstruction" after 1950 in the form of the civil rights movement, in order to fulfill the promises made after the Civil War some eighty years before.

INSTANT

AMERICAN HISTORY

CHAPTER 1

THE NEW WORLD

YOU MUST REMEMBER THIS

For over 500 years a certain Portuguese seafarer (Columbus) has dined out on his trip to the Bahamas, but it was the Native Americans who had first claim to American soil.

IMPORTANT EVENTS

★ First humans arrive in North America, 40,000–15,000 B.C.
★ Pre-Columbian civilizations flourish, 15,000 B.C.–1500 A.D.
★ Leif Eriksson explores North American coast, ca. 1000 A.D.
★ Columbus lands in the Bahamas, 1492
★ Jamestown founded, 1607
★ Virginia colony establishes a legislative assembly, 1619
★ Pilgrims land in the Mayflower and establish a colony at Plymouth, 1620
★ English seize New Netherlands from the Dutch, renaming it New York, 1664
★ Georgia founded in 1732, the last of the thirteen colonies

3

THE AMERICAS BEFORE
THE EUROPEANS CAME

Columbus did not discover America. The Americas were already well populated by the time the first greedy Europeans arrived some 500 years ago to take over. The area of North America that lies south of the Arctic tree line and north of present-day Mexico was home to as many as 5 million Native Americans, while a smaller group, the Inuit, or Eskimos, had the frozen lands that bounded the Arctic Ocean all to themselves.

"I'm not sure what we should do with these boat people."

THE FIRST ASIAN-AMERICANS

The indigenous peoples of North America hailed from Asia—not from Japan, China, Korea, or Vietnam, but from Siberia. They made the arduous trip over what is now the Bering Strait about 15,000 to 40,000 years ago, depending on which text book you believe, joining vast herds of bison, deer, mammoths, wild horses, camels, beaver and other creatures in crossing the mix of land and glacial ice that connected Alaska and what is now the easternmost region of Russia.

Shared physiological characteristics of Native Americans and East Asians confirm that the first human inhabitants of what Europeans called the "New World" were actually from Siberia. Among Mexico's Mayan people for example, some children are born with a rare birthmark at the base of their spine. This mark, which disappears within the first two months after birth, is found elsewhere only among the indigenous people of Siberia.

HUNTING, PICKING BERRIES, AND MAKING LONG TRIPS SOUTH

The earliest Americans were hunters and food gatherers. They had a bit of the wanderlust as well—within a few thousand years, they populated the Americas as far south as the Straits of Magellan at the tip of South America. A multitude of tribes, nations, and confederations blossomed north and south, evolving widely varying languages, political systems, customs, and technologies. In Central America, complex societies with inhabitants numbering in the hundreds of thousands, such as the Aztecs and Mayans, rivaled contemporary Europe in the brilliance and complexity of their art, architecture, technology, and political systems. By 1300 A.D., in the heartland of southern Mexico, the Aztecs had established an empire of five million people ruled by a "Chief of Men" from the lavishly built capital of Tenochtitlan. This was a city of temples, palaces, and market squares that astonished the Spanish conquerors who arrived two centuries later. On the Yucatan peninsula and further south, the Mayan peoples created a distinctive civilization with elaborate religious rituals, and monumental architecture that endures to this day. There was an underside however, a dark side to this grandeur: Both cultures practiced idol worship as well as human sacrifice on a vast scale to appease the gods. It's unlikely that the victims of the distinctive religious custom of sacrifice paused to appreciate the architecture of Tenochtitlan as the priests slit their chests and ripped out their beating hearts.

Further north, in today's United States, there are legions of small tribal groups whose members numbered in the hundreds. The earliest authenticated signs of human presence in the United States consist of stone scrapers, blades, and projectile points found in New Mexico, objects which would one day lead to an entire industry based on exploitation of underfunded anthropologists. These artifacts date from about 8000 B.C., so the first residents of North America clearly knew how to hunt.

None of the Native American peoples who lived north of our present border with Mexico created societies as complex as those that flowered further south under the Aztecs and Mayans. But the achievements of the North American tribes were remarkable nonetheless. Each tribe adapted brilliantly to the ecosystem in which it lived—mountain, desert, forest, plain, or seaboard. Indeed, the yin and yang of humans and nature, which modern America seeks to balance through environmental legislation, was an innate part of the Native American culture.

THE FIVE NORTH AMERICAN GROUPS

Anthropologists divide the Indian cultures of North America, as they existed just before the European intrusion, into five large groupings. The Eastern Woodland tribes lived primarily in a well-watered, densely forested region. They grew vegetables, fished, and hunted, and they played lacrosse without the benefit of NCAA Division I rules. To the west of the Woodland groups were the nomadic Plains tribes, such as the Sioux, Crow, Blackfeet, Comanches, and Cheyenne, who built skin covered teepees and made careers out of farming and hunting bison. Once these Native Americans acquired horses and guns from white pioneers, their productivity as providers improved, as did their talent for making

*A nineteenth-century depiction
of a Native American.*

settlers wish they'd never crossed the Hudson. The Hopi, Zuñi, and Anasazi Indians of the southwest lived in proto-condominiums made of adobe or stone. Their dwellings were clustered into contiguous groups of houses known as pueblos. Late arrivals in this region included the Apache and Navaho. These hardy nomads hunted game, and preyed on Pueblans and visiting Spaniards alike.

NATIVE AMERICANS: A (VERY) QUICK-REFERENCE ATLAS
. . . .
Here are the names of some of the tribes from each of the five large groupings

The Eastern Woodland
   Iroquois, Shawnee, Huron, Delaware, Cherokee
The Plains tribes
   Sioux, Crow, Blackfoot, Comanches, and Cheyenne
The Southwest tribes
   Hopi, Zuñi, Anasazi, Apache, and Navaho
The West Coast Indians
   Chumash, Winton, Hupa, Miwok
Northwest Indians
   Tlingits, Nootkas, Kwakiutls, Tillamooks, Salish, and Chinnooks

---

The West Coast Indians relied on salmon fishing for subsistence; those further inland lived on what today might be called a nouvelle cuisine diet of acorn flour and venison. North of what is now California were the Northwest Indians. Such peoples as the Tlingits, Nootkas and Chinnooks harvested the finned bounty of the sea. Status and wealth played a significant role in the culture of Native Americans of the Northwest. They treasured blankets, canoes, decorated hides and other goods. They divested themselves of their loot at ceremonial bonfires called "potlatches," in which the more material goods you burned, the higher your status in the community. (Which bears a curious similarity to the lifestyles of modern America.)

The effect of the Native American peoples on North American culture is usually underestimated. In the past they were depicted as "painted savages"; wicked enemies of civilization and impediments to the purposeful exploitation of America's natural resources. Native Americans did indeed resist white encroachment, sometimes fiercely. However, in recent decades, historians and the general public have acknowledged that they were more sinned against than sinning. They bowed to a rising tide of migration west, to superior military resources that were brutally applied, and to European diseases against which the Native Americans had no immunity. Despite the unequal relationship between Indians and whites, the complex connection between these two cultures had a part to play in the formation of the American character: individualistic, self-reliant, laconic, and oriented toward action.

SO IF COLUMBUS DIDN'T DISCOVER AMERICA, WHO DID?

Leif Eriksson points to America, which he has just "discovered."

While the schoolbooks glorify Columbus the Admiral of the Ocean Seas, and though from the point of view of "Indians," America didn't need "discovering," other explorers actually sneaked into town before Columbus, and so deserve a share of our attention. The first arrival occurred around 1000

A.D. when Leif Eriksson, a Norse navigator living in Greenland, cruised the northeast coast of North America. He returned home to tout the wonders of "Wineland (Vinland) the Good," where grapes grew large and the streams were chock full of salmon. A few settlements did grow out of his adventures: excavations in the 1960s in northern Newfoundland, the easternmost province of Canada, uncovered a village of eight longhouses laid out just like those found in Greenland, Iceland, and Norway. Some Old World-like implements were discovered there as well.

GOOD FOR SALMON, NOT SO HOT FOR NORSEMEN

It may have been a nice place to visit, but the Vikings either didn't want or weren't able to live there. Norse resources at home were not sufficient to support colonies in faraway places. At the time Eriksson tumbled ashore on Wineland, Europe had been declining in population, wealth, and political cohesion for 500 years. The main legacy of Roman domination in previous eras was a hodge-podge of small decentralized states. Between 1000 and 1500, however, European values and institutions were to undergo revolutionary change. Trade began to revive and with it came the growth of towns as well as a larger and richer merchant class. The continent's rising wealth transformed kingdoms into modern nation-states with armies, navies, bureaucracies, and, of course, tax-collectors. By the opening years of the fifteenth century, Europe was a continent transformed. Commerce, the desire for wealth and treasure, and religious persecution would stimulate migration into previously unimagined realms.

EUROPE EXPANDS

By 1400, the seafaring Portuguese were poised to challenge the world for control of the Eastern spice and luxury trade. Hitherto it had been in the hands of Arabs, Levantines, Venetians and other traders who raised prices to exorbitant levels. How to bypass these middlemen in East-West trade became an urgent problem for the European countries, one not unlike the modern consumer's bid to avoid sales tax on mail order. The renowned navigational skills of Portuguese sea captains enabled the nation's merchant fleet to inch south along the west coast of Africa, probing for a way around the continent and a free path to India and East Asia. They finally found the southern tip of that mysterious continent, a seafarer's landmark now known as the Cape of Good Hope.

HIGH TECH, 15TH-CENTURY VERSION

By 1400, the Portuguese had developed the three-masted caravel, a ship able to deal with ocean currents and winds better than ships designed to sail the Mediterranean. The mariner's compass allowed them to tell directions far from land, and the quadrant and astrolabe gave them a fix on their latitude north or south of the equator. Most important, their ships were equipped with cannons that made them formidable engines of war, and invariably gave them the edge in encounters with Moslem and East Asian rivals. With the help of this new technology, the Portuguese, within 50 years, had wrested the lucrative eastern trade from the Mediterranean middlemen and had established an empire of far-flung commercial posts in Africa, the Persian Gulf, India, China, and Java.

WHO'S
H
O

Do These Names Ring a Bell?

Christopher Columbus (1451–1506).
Italian navigator sailing under the Spanish flag who landed in the Bahamas in 1492.

Sir Francis Drake (1540–1596).
English navigator and pirate, fought the Spanish Armada, explored the West Indies with John Hawkins, and unsuccessfully sought the Northwest Passage.

Sir Humphrey Gilbert (1537–1583).
Half-brother of Sir Walter Raleigh. Founded Newfoundland on his second voyage to the New World, establishing a colony at St. John's.

Sir Walter Raleigh (c.1552–1618).
Courtier, navigator, and poet. Explored Trinidad, the Orinoco River and North Carolina.

William Bradford (1590–1656).
Leader of the small group that arrived in the New World on the Mayflower to found Plymouth Plantation in Massachusetts. Author of *History of Plimoth Plantation,* the first book of American history.

Roger Williams (c.1604–1683).
The separatist Puritan who founded Rhode Island after escaping from the Massachusetts Bay Colony, famous for his excellent relations with the Narraganset Indians. His colony was the first to separate church and state, eliminating the requirement of church membership for voting.

NOW THAT YOU KNOW WHAT COLUMBUS DIDN'T DO, HERE'S WHAT HE DID DO

The other new nation states of Europe chose not to let Portugal monopolize its opulent new trade routes around the Cape of Good Hope. Under the joint rulers Isabella of Castile and Ferdinand of Aragon, Spain too yearned to grow rich. The Spanish crown's agent was a mariner from the city of Genoa in Italy, Christopher Columbus. He was a wool merchant's son, and not surprisingly, a dreamer: He thought the shortest way by sea to the East was due west across the Atlantic. Unaware of the barrier of the Americas, and believing the world was far smaller than it turned out to be (surprise), he presumed that only a few weeks of sailing westward would bring Europeans to the Indies. He had peddled this unlikely idea for years, seeking sponsorship and funding

from virtually every European ruler. Finally, in early 1492, the bold, or perhaps just gullible, Queen Isabella agreed to provide Columbus with ships, crew, and supplies. In return the crown would share in the profits of the voyage. Columbus set sail with three small vessels scarcely bigger than a weekend sport fishing boat plus the kind of crew members you wouldn't take home to mother. That is, many of the lads who joined this voyage

THE FOUR VOYAGES OF COLUMBUS

Columbus just couldn't get enough of the New World, and kept coming back despite the lack of decent accommodations. Here's a quick summary of the four trips:

Columbus, pensive, and his crew, desperate,
just before they "discovered" America.

1. **The First Voyage. The Niña, the Pinta, and the Santa Maria, with a total of 88 men. The Niña and the Pinta each held 18, and the Santa Maria, with Columbus himself in command, had 52. Began Friday, August 3, 1492. Landed at San Salvador (probably Watling Island) on October 12. Left 44 men to build a fort out of the remains of the Santa Maria, which ran aground**

to the edge of the Earth were probably men who saw her majesty's fetid jails as their only alternative. The vessels left Palos in Spain in early August and six weeks later touched land in what is now the Bahamas. The "Admiral" explored the Bahamas and the islands of Cuba and Hispaniola. Believing he had touched lands off the coast of East Asia, Columbus called the inhabitants Indians. He returned to Spain in March, 1493 with cap-

off Hispaniola, and returned to Lisbon aboard the Niña.

2. **The Second Voyage.** Three large caravels and 14 frigates with 1,500 men and all the animals and equipment necessary to start a colony, including 12 missionaries, set out on September 23, 1493. Sighted land on November 3, "discovered" Guadelupe, Antigua, St. Martin, and a dozen other islands. Found the fort erected by members of the first voyage burned, and its inhabitants dispersed. This second expedition gave a hint of things to come: On June 24, 1495, five shiploads of Indians were sent off to Seville to be sold as slaves. Columbus sailed back to Spain, reaching Cadiz on June 11, 1496.

3. **The Third Voyage.** Sailed on May 30, 1498 with six ships (two others had been sent on ahead). Sighted Trinidad, Tobago, Grenada, and Margarita, and, for the first time, saw the coast of South America. But the colonization wasn't going well, and this was the voyage from which poor Columbus was returned in chains after the appointment of a new governor in August, 1500.

4. **The Fourth Voyage.** Restored to favor, Columbus set out one final time on May 9, 1502 with 150 men under his command in four caravels. Sighted land on July 30. He stayed in Jamaica until June 28, 1504. Arrived back in Spain for the final time on November 7.

tive natives, exotic birds and plants, and a little gold. The man who had spent years pitching his scheme to skeptical princes all over Europe was now showered with honors.

From 1493 to 1503, Columbus made three more trips to the Central American coast and the Caribbean Basin, areas that he incorrectly referred to as the Indies. He charted the islands of the Caribbean and combed the bays, peninsulas, and river mouths of the Americas in search of a passage to Asia. In a few hundred years, the Panama canal would have solved his problems, but as it was, he never did find the far-eastern spices and gold for which he'd quested. Glory on Earth can be fleeting. Though the pioneer navigator figures preeminently in today's accounts of the period, the achievements of other New World explorers would in time divert the public eye. Columbus died in relative obscurity, though his story has since become mother's milk for generations of textbook writers. Happily for citizens of the U.S.A. his voyages spurred other Spanish conquistadors and explorers to follow his lead, exploring every cranny of the two American continents. By 1500 or so, roving journalists like Amerigo Vespucci, a Florentine who accompanied several Spanish captains in trans-Atlantic voyages, began to describe the western lands as a "new world," rather than an extension of Asia. For all of Columbus's trouble, the mapmakers named the new lands after Amerigo instead of the man whose deeds earn some of us a day off every October.

AND NOW EVERYONE WANTS TO GET INTO THE ACT

The riches of "the Indies" made Spain the greatest power in Europe and stimulated the envy of the other European nations, who refused to accept Spain's claim to exclusive rights in the New World. Before long, explorers from England, France, and Holland discovered new territories along the eastern shores of the present-day U.S. and Canada, enhancing the Old World's knowledge of the wild lands across the sea.

BEHIND THE SCENES

Little-Known Players and Unsung Heroes

People, few of them white males, who don't always make it into the history books.

Nathaniel Bacon (c.1642–1676).
Leader of an uprising in 1676 against the Governor of the Virginia Colony, the most serious challenge to royal authority until the Revolution—and it was a rebellion in which black slaves and white servants participated side by side.

John Rolfe (1585–1622).
The developer of tobacco as an export crop in the Jamestown colony. Husband of Pocahontas.

Pedro Cabral (c.1467–c.1520).
The Portuguese navigator who accidentally discovered Brazil in 1500.

Pocahontas (c.1596–1617).
The rescuer of John Smith, and the wife of John Rolfe, her marriage helped preserve the peace between colonists and local Indians.

Squanto (?–1622).
The Indian who taught the Pilgrims how to plant corn and fish. He learned English during a forced trip to Europe in 1615, later returning to his native land.

BEHIND THE SCENES

(*continued*)

John Cabot (1425–c.1500).
Genoese captain who explored the coast of North America for King Henry VII of England, searching for a Northwest passage, 1497.

Samuel de Champlain (1567–1635).
Founder of Quebec in 1608.

Henry Hudson (c.1550–1611).
English explorer who, sailing for the Dutch West India Company, discovered the Hudson River Valley, 1609.

George Calvert, Lord Baltimore (c.1580–1632).
Founder of the colony of Maryland, 1632, which was inherited by his son, Cecil, the 2nd Lord Baltimore.

James Oglethorpe (1696–1785).
Head of the board of trustees that founded the Georgia colony for debtors in 1732 at Savannah with 120 settlers.

Anne Hutchinson (c.1590–1643).
A religious woman, mother of thirteen children, she defied church and government in the Massachusetts Bay Colony by asserting that a woman was as capable as a man of interpreting the Bible. She was banished from the colony, and moved to Rhode Island, and then to Long Island, where she was killed by Indians.

WHY THE ENGLISH LEFT HOME

Though England had been in on the ground floor of European exploration of the New World, the Brits dropped out for about sixty years. Then, in 1558, Elizabeth Tudor became Queen Elizabeth, and English energies were unleashed once again. The emigrants from the British Isles did not abandon their ancestral homes without reason. Indeed, they had strong inducements to

Elizabeth I (1533–1603), looking at least virginal enough to have Virginia named after her.

cross the dangerous Atlantic in frail wooden ships and plant themselves in a tangled wilderness of savages and wild beasts. Farmers, displaced by the spread of sheep grazing, turned to America as a place where they could acquire land, and younger sons of gentlemen, deprived of land by inheritance laws that awarded all land to a family's first born son (the rule of primogeniture), crossed the Atlantic to establish their own estates. Merchants followed these emigrants to trade in fish, furs, timber, tobacco, and rice.

SHOW 'EM HOW CLEVER YOU ARE
....

Here's one your friends will never get. Henry VIII, was famous for having six wives. And most people know that Elizabeth I was Henry's daughter. But which of the six wives was her mother? Think about it while you finish reading this page. Then check out the next box.

Beyond these economic motives, British settlers also came for freedom of conscience. During the reign of Queen Elizabeth's father, Henry VIII, England experienced a religious revolution that was part of the Protestant Reformation sweeping northern Europe. The Protestant reformers, inspired by Germany's Martin Luther, condemned the worldliness and corruption of the Renaissance Catholic Church. England remained securely Catholic until 1534, when King Henry, who'd been denied a divorce by the Pope, broke with Catholicism and made himself head of a new Church of England. Soon, loyal Catholics, Protestants of the Church of England, and an even stricter breed of Protestants—the Calvinists—were at odds. Queen Elizabeth sought a middle way between the Puritans and the Catholics, but after her death in 1603, the Stuart kings, James I and Charles I were unable to contain this killing field of spiritual enmities. Thus the religious radicals of the seventeenth and eighteenth centuries found a mood of intolerance in their own backyard that made the rigors of the New World seem inviting.

THE ANSWER

Right! Anne Boleyn, wife number 2, was Liz's Mom! But you get no credit if you remember it only because you saw the movie. You may also remember that Henry married Anne without taking the preliminary step of divorcing Catherine, his first wife. But he was King, after all, and he arranged to have that first marriage annulled. Anne Boleyn's unpleasant personality, adulterous adventures, and, worst of all, her inability to produce a living male child eventually made her lose her head— literally. And Henry married Jane Seymour the very next day! These people make Fergie and Di and Andy and Charles look positively regal by comparison.

THE EARLY ENGLISH SETTLEMENTS

Queen Elizabeth at first did little to encourage English overseas enterprise. Spain claimed much of the New World and the Queen was reluctant to challenge the country that had grown powerful on the gold and silver of Mexico and Peru. By the 1580s, however, the Queen began to encourage her sea captains Sir Francis Drake and Sir John Hawkins to attack Spanish ships on the high seas. She also granted charters to Sir Humphrey Gilbert and his half-brother Sir Walter Raleigh to establish settlements in the lands now known as Newfoundland and Virginia. The latter region, located on the Atlantic coast of North America, was named after Elizabeth, the Virgin Queen. Both ventures came to grief as settlers could not manage to provide for themselves in the wilderness. The outposts were quickly abandoned.

FIRST YOU GET TO BE KING. THEN YOU GET A NEW COLONY AND A MOSQUITO-INFESTED RIVER NAMED AFTER YOU

The first successful English colony in America was the Jamestown settlement of 1607, established after Elizabeth's death by the Virginia Company, a joint stock company made up of merchants, "gentlemen," and philanthropists from London and Plymouth interested in exploiting the furs and fish of North America and in providing a haven for England's surplus population. In 1607 the company sent out two expeditions to America, one to Maine, the other to Virginia. The Maine colony quickly expired through an inability to live off the land. The Virginia colony, situated along the James River, survived and became the first permanent English settlement in North America.

THE LEGEND OF JOHN SMITH

Pocahontas saves the neck of Captain John Smith.

Compared to John Smith, Indiana Jones is just an Old Man in a Rocking Chair. The romantic bit with Pocahontas, the Indian maiden who reportedly saved his skin, was the least of it. John Smith led the kind of life they write about in boys' adventure stories—went to sea at 16, led the colonization of Jamestown at 26, explored wild rivers, and bravely fought the Indians. He was falsely accused of murder and was actually sentenced to be hanged, but gained a reprieve at the last minute. He explored the Chesapeake Bay and its tributaries, getting so badly stung by a stingray at one point that he returned to Jamestown to be treated by a surgeon. Smith managed amidst all this to collect enough data to write a careful narrative of the expedition and draw a remarkably accurate map. In 1614, he explored the New England coast from Penobscot to Cape Cod, once again drawing a splendid map. In 1615, on an unsuccessful expedition to establish a colony in New England, he was captured by pirates and later released. In his spare time, he kept busy by writing and publishing half a dozen books on history, geography, and his own adventures. And he crammed it all into a life that lasted just 52 years.

Unfortunately, Jamestown was in mosquito-infested country and the settlers were ravaged by malaria; people died in droves. Rampant disease might merely have hastened the inevitable for some of these immigrants. They were mainly soft handed gentlemen with a greater appetite for finding gold than working hard and planting crops that might actually stave off starvation. The leader of their expedition, Captain John Smith, forced the idlers to work and the colony just barely survived.

THE DAWN OF LUNG CANCER IN AMERICA; A PRIMER.

In 1612, an enterprising settler, John Rolfe (who later married Pocahontas) began to sow tobacco, an Indian plant which he improved by selective breeding. British pipe smokers liked it, and were willing to pay premium prices. The money rolled in. Before long Virginia settlers were growing the "stinking weed" on every patch of ground they could find, including the streets of Jamestown itself. Sailors arriving in Virginia jumped ship to get in on the bonanza. Prices soon fell to more reasonable levels but by that time the planters had established a firm economy built on smoke.

THE FIRST SIGNS OF DEMOCRACY IN THE NEW WORLD

The stimulus of the tobacco trade helped the Virginia colony to evolve rapidly during the seventeenth century. In 1619, the company established an assembly of resident males with power to pass laws. This was the seed that later grew into the Virginia House of Burgesses, the first representative body in America. In 1622, Virginia experienced a devastating attack by the local Indians under chief Opecancenough, a blow precipitated by English intrusion on Indian lands. Three hundred and forty-seven settlers died. The colonists retaliated and virtually exterminated the Indian tribes of Virginia's coastal areas (a region known as the "Tidewater"). In 1624 the company lost its charter, that is, its crown-given license to attempt commercial development. Thereafter Virginia became a royal colony which in subsequent years would be administered by governors whom the crown chose to appoint. Such leaders governed with the advice and assistance of the Virginia Burgesses, which functioned as a small parliament.

LOTS OF WORK, AND
NO ONE TO DO IT

Virginia's troubles were by no means over. Disease took a high toll of settlers. To offset the losses, a small, steady stream of immigrants continued to arrive each year, and the settlement gradually expanded out from Jamestown in concentric rings. Not until the ratio of women to men began to even up late in the seventeenth century did population grow by natural increase—the excess of births over deaths.

For a long time the Virginia colony and the other colonies that soon followed, suffered a severe labor shortage. Everywhere in early America there was endless work to do—clearing, building, plowing, cultivating, harvesting, hunting, fishing—and few people to do it. In the plantation colonies south of Pennsylvania, labor shortages kept growers of tobacco, rice, indigo, and other commercial crops, from making the profits they desired.

Meanwhile, in England, thousands of landless men and husbandless women collected in the crowded towns or wandered the countryside in search of work. To attract such people, several colonies established the "headright" system, which granted each settler who came at his own expense 50 acres of free land and another 50 for each settler he brought with him. This plan failed to fulfill the colonies' needs and so an alternative arose: An English laborer could sign a contract ("indenture") with a ship captain or recruiting agent in exchange for passage to the New World. Upon arrival the indenture was sold to a planter or other employer and the worker served his master for four years or so. At the end of the contract, the man was released, usually with some "freedom dues" such as a gift of clothes, equipment, and even at times, some land.

AFRICA AND AMERICA

Thousands of indentured servants came to the Chesapeake and Carolina colonies. But even so labor shortages persisted and by the middle of the seventeenth century the planters began to import black slaves from West Africa, primarily from the region of present-day Senegal and Gambia south to Angola.

This stretch of sub-Saharan Africa was densely populated when the Portuguese first crept southward along its coastline. African achievement in seafaring, the arts, education, and politics rivaled those of western and far eastern cultures. Amid such achievement, however, there existed a centuries-old slave trade. Since Roman times, if not before, Arab and other traders had shipped their human cargo throughout the Middle East and beyond. The scale of the traffic in human flesh increased dramatically, though, with the development of agriculture in the New World. Unfortunately, the African peoples were not united and were unprepared to resist traders from Europe who offered gifts while planning mass abductions. The boom in the slave trade wrenched thousands of innocent people from their homelands and brought them to the Americas to work the tobacco and rice plantations of the mainland and the sugar plantations of the Caribbean islands and South America. Many more black slaves were transported to Jamaica, Cuba, Brazil, Barbados, and Puerto Rico than to the Chesapeake and the Carolinas. But enough were brought to the mainland so that by 1750 there were about 235,000 slaves in the British mainland colonies, almost a quarter of the total population. Once kidnapped by press gangs or bought by African middlemen, and assembled near the coast, the slaves were packed aboard small vessels, and carried to America on the infamous "middle passage." Sanitation aboard "slavers" was notoriously poor, and disheartened and frightened Africans were prone to suicide

WEST AFRICA IN THE SEVENTEENTH CENTURY

West Africa was densely populated when the Portuguese began to explore the coast. Its people were farmers who grew millet, wheat, cassava, fruits, and vegetables; fishermen whose great canoes ranged the Atlantic shore for edible sea creatures; and artisans who fashioned tools, weapons, and art objects of iron, wood, copper, and ivory. Many of the masks, sculpture, and other artifacts of the West African peoples, especially of Benin and Dahomey, are among the glories of the world of art. For a time Gao, Walata, and Timbuktu in the Sudan became intellectual centers with schools equivalent to Western universities. The West African peoples also developed complex social and political systems that rivaled the empires of Europe of the East. Ghana, Mali, and Songhay were large kingdoms whose rulers' sway ranged over thousands of square miles and many different peoples.

or, when opportunity offered, violent rebellion. Still, most of the enchained Africans arrived intact and found ready sale to the planters who gathered at the docks to purchase "likely Negroes" for their fields.

In the mainland colonies, black workers were at first treated as indentured servants and permitted their freedom after a period of years. But this arrangement soon gave way to permanent "chattel slavery." Under this system, slaves and their offspring were the property of their owners, and like other property could be bought, sold, bequeathed, and inherited. The economic advantages of slave labor were so great that the institution eventually eclipsed indentured servitude. Slave populations on the mainland grew fast in the eighteenth century, partially due to importation but also through natural increase.

RELIGION AND SETTLEMENT

You will recall that after the death of Queen Elizabeth in 1603, England underwent a period of religious intolerance under the Stuart kings, James I and Charles I. The most severe persecution of Protestant dissenters in England did not occur until the 1630s, but even before that time, in the early 1600s, a small group of radical Calvinists concluded that the Church of England was beyond purification and had to be abandoned entirely. In 1609, a group of these "Separatists" moved to Leyden, Holland, where they hoped they could live in peace, away from the intolerant orthodoxy that prevailed in their native land. As the years passed, however, the hardships of earning a living and the increased spiritual backsliding of their young led elders of the Separatist church to consider the hazardous journey to America. In 1620, these "Pilgrims" struck a bargain with a group of London merchants to move to lands owned by the Virginia

Company. In exchange for transportation and real estate, they agreed to work for the venture's promoters for seven years. In this roundabout way, religious persecution propelled thousands of English to America and helped populate the new community.

YOU REMEMBER THE PILGRIMS? WELL, HERE'S THE REAL STORY

In September 1620, thirty-five of the Separatists, joined by other adventuresome Englanders, departed from Plymouth, England in a small vessel named, as you learned every year from second grade through sixth, the Mayflower. Their destination had been Virginia. But they must have taken a wrong turn somewhere, because they made their landfall in what is now Massachusetts. Weary of travel, the Pilgrims decided to settle on the shores of Massachusetts Bay, a body of water protected by the sheltering arm of Cape Cod.

The Mayflower, the ship your ancestors didn't come over on.

THE PLYMOUTH ROCK'S EARLIEST VISITORS: THE PILGRIMS OR THE PLYMOUTH CHAMBER OF COMMERCE?

It's not clear that anyone from the Mayflower ever stepped from a boat onto Plymouth Rock, and the poor boulder has been moved more than once as its prominence in the books has waxed and waned. Today, the fenced-in rock that you see by the seashore is at the very least an inspiring touchstone (as it were) of our Pilgrim ancestry. In truth, a chain of anecdotes (beginning with the testimony of an Old Man who was but a boy when he heard the story from another Old Man. . . .) are all that link us with the true role of the rock. Perhaps the only thing we can be certain of is that the rock used to be bigger, in the days before local tourist authorities erected a protective monument around it to protect their patrimony from the chisels and hammers of tourists wanting a chip off the old block.

The little settlement named Plymouth grew through natural increase and modest immigration from England. This became known as the Pilgrim "Old Colony." It eventually merged with Massachusetts in 1691. Free enterprise still thrives there today: An historical re-creation of the settlement, complete with costumed men and women taking on the roles of the original citizens, now harvests each year a healthy crop of tourist dollars.

Back in England, a much larger group of Protestant dissenters prepared to flee England. These Puritans had long hoped to reform the Church of England from within, but by the early 1620s when a new wave of Anglican repression began, they had begun to lose heart, and so developed a stomach for sea travel.

The great Puritan migration began in 1630 when four vessels disembarked 400 men, women, and children, with all their supplies, household goods, and equipment at Charlestown and several other spots along Massachusetts Bay. Their intrepid leader was John Winthrop, a gentleman (though also a lawyer), who'd concluded there was no future for him and other pious folk in England. He believed that in America, God's people could establish a virtuous "city upon a hill" which all Christians might take for a model. Winthrop and his companions brought with them the charter of the Massachusetts Bay Colony so that the new community might rule itself rather than be governed by the company directors back in England.

The initial emigrants were soon joined by others. As persecution accelerated in Britain, more and more Puritans abandoned their homeland and made sail for America. From the outset this movement consisted primarily of whole families, not single men as was the case in Virginia. The newcomers included a broad spectrum of English society. Most of them were farmers and laborers but many were ministers, lawyers, doctors, and graduates of Cambridge University. By 1690, Massachusetts Bay counted 50,000 residents, almost as many as Virginia, though the latter colony had been established years earlier.

THE NEW ENGLAND COLONIES

All but one of the communities that eventually became the original thirteen colonies were founded during the seventeenth century. In New England, Connecticut and Rhode Island were settled primarily by people who disagreed with the Puritan leaders. Though the Puritan grandees were themselves refugees from persecution, they had no qualms about harassing those who disagreed with their religious views. New Hampshire, which became a separate royal colony in 1679, was founded by emigrants from Massachusetts seeking cheap land.

THE DUTCH IN THE NEW WORLD

South of New England were the middle colonies of New York, New Jersey, Pennsylvania, and Delaware. The first was established by the Dutch West India Company, a joint-stock firm of Netherlands merchants interested in trading furs with the Indians. In 1623 the company created settlements on Manhattan Island and near the site of what is now Albany. The Dutch outposts grew slowly and to encourage emigration the company granted rich gentlemen, who would agree to transport fifty people to America, enormous estates along the Hudson. These they could rule as feudal lords (patroons), just as Donald Trump might be said to preside over Atlantic City today. New Netherlands never achieved much more than modest success. If the company's inventors had been able to hold onto their land for just a couple of centuries more, New Yorkers would now be wearing clogs to work. In 1664 the Dutch possessions were seized by the English who considered the Dutch settlers a "nest of interlopers" and renamed New York, after its "proprietor," the King's brother, the Duke of York.

DROP THAT COCKTAIL, STOP THAT CONVERSATION! NEW AMSTERDAM LIVES!

You may not see anyone marching around in wooden shoes, and there are very few windmills around New York, but the Dutch have left a rich legacy of resonant names from Peekskill, the Tappan Zee, and the Catskills upstate to the Bronx and Staten Island in New York City. If you live in or even visit the Big Apple, you may astound your friends or unnerve strangers by casually noting the Dutch origin of all of the following familiar New York names: Spuyten Duyvil, the Bowery, Block Island, Amsterdam Avenue, Stuyvesant Avenue, New Dorp, Todt Hill, New Utrecht, Kill Van Kull, Van Cortlandt Park, Dyckman Street, Van Nostrand Avenue, Gansevoort Street, Gouverneur Lane, Beekman Place, Harlem, and Broadway (the Dutch called it the "breedeweg").

For the Same Low Price: An Extra Conversation Stopper: Tell them that the Holland Tunnel has nothing to do with the Dutch at all—it was named after Clifford M. Holland, the chief engineer on the project who died while it was under construction.

HE'D RATHER BE IN PHILADELPHIA

Pennsylvania was founded in the early 1680s by William Penn, an English Quaker, who sought a refuge for his persecuted coreligionists. Under his charter from Charles II, Penn ruled as a feudal "proprietor" but the colony's generous laws and cheap land attracted not only Quakers but German Protestants as well. It soon became a prosperous community of farmers and merchants trading with Britain and the Caribbean. By the middle of the eighteenth century, Philadelphia was the largest town in British America. The little colony of Delaware, originally settled by Swedes, was part of the Penn grant and did not split off until 1701. New Jersey too had a Quaker origin, though many New Englanders and other non-Quakers settled in the portion of the colony adjacent to New York.

WILLIAM PENN

William Penn was not your average sort of guy. At the age of 12, he had a religious epiphany during which he experienced profound "inward comfort" combined with a conviction of "an external glory in the room." He converted to Quakerism while at Oxford, and though his father must have realized by this time that he had a rather unusual kid, he nevertheless was so angered by this that he whipped, beat, and turned young William out of the house. Fortunately, the elder Penn cooled down and the two reconciled. William Penn grew up to become a soldier, a poet, a biographer, a theologian, a member of parliament, a preacher, a Fellow of the Royal Society, and the inheritor through his wife's family of a large estate. He asked for, and received from the King, a large grant of land in America—Pennsylvania—over which he became the supreme governor, guiding the colony to prosperity.

THE COLONIES TO THE SOUTH

Maryland, Virginia's Chesapeake Bay neighbor, was founded by Lord Baltimore, an English Catholic nobleman who, like Penn, sought a haven from religious persecution. Baltimore and his heirs tried to establish a feudal principality on the Chesapeake with manor lords, tenants, and baronial courts, but for reasons that would have been obvious to anyone but an inbred aristocrat, the system soon broke down. (Would you respond to an invitation to undertake a terrifying sea voyage, followed by a life of toil under the same kind of ostentatious pinheads you already lived beneath at home?) Few wanted to come to a colony that did not offer liberal laws and the chance to become a freeholder. Nor did Maryland's role as a Catholic refuge endure. Eventually Anglicans became the majority and repealed laws that had codified religious tolerance in the colony. Maryland nonetheless flourished economically, mirroring Virginia's success as a land of slave-worked tobacco plantations.

The colonies to the south of Virginia, with the exception of North Carolina, followed the pattern of the Old Dominion as producers of staple crops for export based on slave labor. South Carolina was settled in 1669–70 by people from England from the English Caribbean island of Barbados. The first colonists established Charlestown (Charleston) and soon were producing good crops of corn, livestock, and dairy products. Rice was introduced about 1690 and rice plantations along the tidal waters worked by black slaves soon became the chief source of the colony's wealth. North Carolina was settled largely by spillover population from Virginia. Unlike its aristocratic southern neighbor it remained a society of poor, unruly farmers working small spots of land.

Georgia, founded in 1732, was the last of the thirteen colonies. It had a dual purpose: a buffer against Spanish Florida and a haven for imprisoned debtors. It succeeded as a military outpost but not as a philanthropic enterprise. Despite the efforts of its founder, James Oglethorpe, to exclude slavery, the settlers quickly concluded that without slaves they could not prosper and therefore pressured the "trustees" to relent. In 1750 the law prohibiting slavery was repealed and Georgia became a slave-worked plantation colony like its neighbor, South Carolina.

THE THIRTEEN FAMOUS ORIGINAL

By the 1730s, the roster of the original thirteen colonies was complete. In that year the British mainland colonies (excluding Nova Scotia) had a population of about 630,000 people who mostly clung to the coast. The overwhelming majority of them engaged in agricultural pursuits. Most Americans were descendants of the earliest English settlers, but a sizeable minority, some 90,000 people, were black. Furthermore, an ever larger proportion of new arrivals sailed from Germany, Scotland, and Northern Ireland. And this was a population growing more quickly than almost any in the world. The population of colonial America doubled every twenty-five years owing to a combination of immigration and natural increase, both encouraged by abundant land, good nutrition, lightly imposed government (and much later, in the 1950s, the wanton atmosphere of the drive-in movie theater). As of 1760, about 1.6 million people lived in the thirteen colonies. America was on its way to becoming a vigorous and mature community.

SUMMARY

⏱ Civilizations as sophisticated as the ones in Europe flourished in North and South America a thousand years before Columbus's arrival. Regardless of what they told you in grade school, Columbus didn't discover America.

⏱ Pursuit of the spice and luxury trade motivated the seafaring nations of Europe, especially Spain and Portugal, to sail toward the West.

⏱ Religious persecution in Europe and desire for commercial gain in the New World was the impetus for the European settlements in America.

⏱ A combination of generous government spending and private business investment brought settlers to the New World.

⏱ By 1730, the original thirteen colonies were well established in North America, and by 1760, there were more than 1.6 million Europeans living in them.

CHAPTER 2

INDEPENDENCE

YOU MUST REMEMBER THIS

Tea is one thing, the exploitation of a vast rich continent is quite another. The War of Independence was fought for life, liberty, and the pursuit of happiness, but it was also fought for money.

IMPORTANT EVENTS

★ French and Indian War, 1758–1763
★ The Stamp Act, 1765
★ The Boston Tea Party and the Intolerable Acts, 1773
★ The Shot Heard 'Round the World, 1775
★ The Declaration of Independence, 1776
★ Burgoyne's Surrender at Saratoga, 1777
★ The Articles of Confederation, 1781
★ Cornwallis's Surrender at Yorktown, 1781
★ The Treaty of Paris, 1783

To Britain, the American colonies were a source of two things: wealth and trouble. And the Americans felt the same about the British. Out of this mutual skepticism and distrust, the U.S.A. was born.

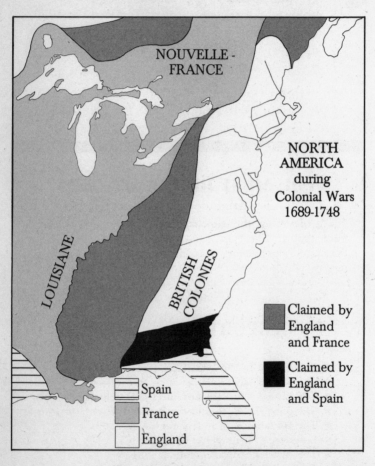

NOUVELLE-FRANCE

NORTH AMERICA during Colonial Wars 1689-1748

LOUISIANE

BRITISH COLONIES

Claimed by England and France

Claimed by England and Spain

Spain

France

England

This map depicts the North American colonies, pre-Revolution.

**WHO'S
WHO**
☞

Do These Names Ring a Bell?

❦ **Sam Adams** (1722–1803).
Chief agitator at the Boston Tea Party in 1773, delegate to the Continental Congress, and signer of the Declaration of Independence. He was John Adams's second cousin.

❦ **John Hancock** (1737–1793).
President of the Continental Congress, signer of the Declaration of Independence.

❦ **Benjamin Franklin** (1706–1790).
Statesman, inventor, publisher, printer, Postmaster General, scientist. Signer of the Declaration of Independence and participant in the Constitutional Convention.

❦ **Thomas Paine** (1737–1809).
An English radical, a poor immigrant who arrived in America in 1774, his pamphlet *Common Sense: Addressed to the Inhabitants of America,* published in 1776, urged rebellion against the British monarch.

❦ **Thomas Gage** (1721–1787).
Commander-in-Chief of British forces in America (1763–72); sent a force to seize arms from colonists at Concord. He was in command at Bunker Hill, after which he was relieved of his command.

❦ **Benedict Arnold** (1741–1801).
Soldier and turncoat, he tried to betray West Point to the British, after which he became an officer in the British army.

WHO'S WHO

☛

(*continued*)

🐾 **John Burgoyne** (1722–1792).
English soldier and dramatist. Defeated at Saratoga in 1777 by Horatio Gates.

🐾 **Horatio Gates** (1728–1806).
English-born American soldier, the victor at Saratoga in 1777.

🐾 **Charles Cornwallis** (1738–1805).
After many successful campaigns in America, he was defeated at Yorktown and forced to surrender, in what was a decisive battle of the revolutionary war.

DEMOCRACY, YES,
BUT WHITE MALES ONLY

By 1750, each of the colonies had its own legislature with two houses, the upper house, whose members were appointed by the governor, and the lower house, elected by white male property owners (who usually had to have the right religion, too). Though not exactly a democracy by today's standards, it was a lot more democratic than any other eighteenth century government. These legislatures were not completely on their own—the royal governor, appointed by the King of England, could still veto whatever laws they passed—but members could take up almost any question they wanted to, and pass laws at least pertaining to local matters with tacit approval from abroad.

But what about the larger world? Were the colonies

supposed to help make imperial policy? Deal with foreign enemies? Pay taxes to support the empire? When the colonies were small, no one much cared. But now they were bigger and wealthier, and much harder to ignore. In fact, each colony began to assume the kind of corporate ego we now associate with the owners of major league baseball teams, and likewise adopted a recalcitrant manner with the enthroned "commissioner" (i.e. the King) back in England.

THE IMPERIAL ECONOMY

Britain wanted to use the colonies for its own purposes—that is, the colonies were to be an integral part of the larger plan that the mercantilists had laid out, wherein

BEHIND THE SCENES

Little-Known Players and Unsung Heroes

People, few of them white males, who don't always make it into the history books.

Abigail Adams (1744–1818).
Wife of John Adams, and manager of his properties when he was absent on business.

Pontiac (1720–1769).
Chief of the Ottawa, organizer of what the settlers called a "conspiracy" to drive whites back east across the Appalachians. After much fighting, finally made peace with the British in 1766.

Crispus Attucks (c.1723–1770).
Attucks, a worker, was the first person killed in the Boston Massacre, when British troops fired on a crowd of ropemakers protesting British rule.

economic interests on each side of the Atlantic complemented the needs of the other. After all, England's mercantilists were the ones who'd inspired colonization in the first place. The spoils ought to be Britain's. Logical, maybe, but perhaps just a bit unrealistic.

RULES ARE EASY TO FOLLOW WHEN YOU'RE THE ONE MAKING THE RULES

In the previous century, Parliament had passed the Navigation Acts. These laws and regulations were designed to make sure that Britain profited from all colonial trade. In economic terms, mankind had finally found a legal way to squeeze blood out of a turnip. For example, foreigners were excluded from most imperial trade and what could be shipped to the colonies had to pass through Britain first. Conversely, certain goods that the colonies sent abroad were "enumerated," that is they had to pass through Britain before they could be shipped to their final destination in a third country. The British weren't shy about enforcing these strictures. A hive of customs officials swarmed over goods in transit at all the major colonial ports.

The mother country's self-serving trade laws did offer an occasional advantage for Americans. For instance, keeping economic activity within the colonial family meant that shipwrights in the New World snagged a large share of the Empire's shipbuilding business. Yet when it came time for Americans to ship "enumerated" goods to France or Germany—tobacco and rice, for example—their customers had to pay more for everything because duties had to be paid in a British port and that meant less would be sold. The advantages of the system for Britain were clear; the Americans, on the other hand, knew an unfair system of trade when they saw it.

FIGHTING AGAINST THE FRENCH

Paying outlandish duties on trade in tobacco or rice was one thing. Paying for imperial defense was another. For almost two centuries, the colonies had been a killing ground for the European powers, with the French and British (and various allied Indians) doing most of the dying. The British colonists viewed New France (Canada) as a menace—there weren't that many Canadians compared to the number of British, but they were armed to the teeth and loaded for bear (of which there were quite a few in those days).

Trouble first started in the 1670s, with fighting up in the north in Hudson's Bay, over the fur trade. As the end of the century drew nigh, the ubiquitous French began to settle the Mississippi Valley—Louisiane, as they called it. This action was an unsubtle challenge to the British claim that the King owned the entire neighborhood, "from ocean to ocean." (On the positive side, it held out the promise of some decent regional cooking.)

Between 1689 and 1754, Britain and France fought each other in four wars. Each time, France's Indian allies attacked frontier settlements in New England and New York. The most bitter of these conflicts, and the most decisive, was the French and Indian War of 1754–63— the one we all remember, even if we've forgotten the other three. This war commenced with France's massacre of a group of American traders at Pickawillany in present-day Ohio. The French felt this area belonged to them, and had chosen a memorable way to say "get off my property." In response, the well-meaning, if ineffective, governor of Virginia, Robert Dinwiddie, sent 150 men led by the young militia colonel George Washington (remember that name for later) to fortify the region against further attack. The French promptly fell on his group and captured every one of them.

All this activity on the far side of the Appalachians was unnerving to the British, who in 1755 sent an army under General Edward Braddock to protect the interests of their American subjects. On July 8, 1,400 British redcoats plus 450 Americans under George Washington met a smaller force of French and Indians on an open plain near what is now Pittsburgh. What ensued mimicked the line of scrimmage follies of a doormat team in the National Football League. The front rank of the British-American force fired their muskets, and then stepped back to let the second rank fire theirs. Unfortunately, the second rank stumbled right into the first. While the soldiers in red were sorting themselves out, the French, who knew an opportunity when they saw one, shot the British troops to pieces. The sons of France managed to slaughter most of them, including General Braddock himself, and the ones still able to run took off posthaste for homebase. Only 500 redcoats and Americans made it safely back to their base at Fort Cumberland.

Over the next eight years, France and England grappled with each other around the world wherever their colonial interests clashed. At first, the Anglo-Americans kept coming up short, but under the leadership of British prime minister William Pitt, their luck changed. In late 1758, the British finally took Fort Duquesne, the target of General Braddock's earlier failed campaign. The next year a British-American army under General James Wolfe crawled up the cliffs below Canada's Quebec city and defeated the French army led by the Marquis de Montcalm, on the nearby Plains of Abraham. The successes continued, and by 1760, all of Canada was in British hands. Responsibility for Britain's overall victory against the French in North America can be laid to

THE PEACE OF PARIS (FEBRUARY 1763)

This treaty gave Britain all of Canada plus the territory in the Mississippi-Ohio Valley that the French had previously claimed. It also took Florida from Spain, France's ally (with, one suspects, a secret covenant granting Orlando to a future race of Walt Disney walking plush toys). The part of Louisiana west of the Mississippi was not included in this arrangement—it had been earlier ceded by France to Spain—but practically speaking, France had been expelled from North America (except for some Caribbean Islands). For the first time since the English-speaking colonies had been founded, they would not face a French menace from the north.

one man: William Pitt, whose brilliant leadership from afar, and a knack for choosing smart young officers won the day. The French were out-generalled, and in 1763 signed a treaty, the Peace of Paris.

BRITISH-AMERICAN TRIUMPH—AND THE SEEDS OF BRITISH DEFEAT

The Anglo-American victory, ironically, was the seed bed of American independence. With the French peril removed, the Americans felt safer and more free to defy the British. The war had also pumped up Americans' confidence in their organizational and military ability. They had seen the best soldiers and commanders of France and Britain and were underwhelmed.

Britain, having just spent 140 million pounds to defend the colonists, was dismayed to learn that the colonists had often aided the enemy when a profit could be

Chief Pontiac confronts British officers.

made. Other factors added to the consternation of leaders in London: The French did not readily act on the terms of their expulsion, and the Native American Indians were not exactly forming "Welcome Wagons" to greet the settlers who migrated west.

The French defeat left Anglo-American fur traders free to cross the Appalachians, and free as well to further bully and cheat the Native Americans. The eclipse of France also gave settlers in search of a little *lebensraum* (literally, German for "living room") the chance to displace tribes of the Ohio Valley. Early in the summer of 1763, the cork flew off the bottle when these tribes took to the war path under the leadership of Chief Pontiac of the Ottawa tribe. They overran military posts, murdered settlers, and burned cabins. Not until September 1764 were they finally suppressed. For several reasons, then, a continued British military presence in America would be quite necessary, and quite expensive.

The British saw a growing need to appease the Indians and allow time to establish rational policy for western settlement (the phrase "rational policy for western settlement" may, depending on your point of view, be translated as "a well-organized scheme for taking land away from the Indians and distributing it among European settlers"). The British government, under the Proclamation of 1763, drew a line along the Appalachians beyond which white settlement would not be allowed until further notice. However, the paranoid American colonists figured this was just a sly attempt to exclude them from the riches of the West, and to line the pockets of British land speculators. The colonial response was to play fast and loose with the exact location of the boundary, and to put pressure on British representatives to rescind the border decree. By 1774, the disputes with Native Americans over land entered a new improved phase.

SOMEONE'S GONNA HAVE
TO PAY FOR THIS

The British realized it would be necessary to maintain a permanent garrison in America to protect their interests in the New World. England had a long experience with the maintenance of permanent garrisons throughout its Empire and had a repertoire of methods for paying the bills for such troops. The British passed the Sugar Act in 1764. This was not a Las Vegas-style revue but new high duties on foreign nations' exports to the colonies, most notably sugar.

The Stamp Act of 1765 was even worse. Under its provisions all legal documents, plus newspapers, diplomas, dice, playing cards, almanacs had to carry a stamp costing from 2 pence to six pounds. The proceeds from this

---

TAXATION WITHOUT REPRESENTATION:
A SHORT COURSE
. . . .
You know the phrase. Here are the facts. The three laws a colonist has to remember . . . to know when he's getting shafted:

The Sugar Act (1764).
Exorbitant duties on imports, especially on sugar.

The Stamp Act (1764).
Taxes legal documents, diplomas, newspapers, playing cards, and dice. You have to buy the stamps and stick them on, which makes this levy a hard one to dodge— so hard in fact that many countries, including Great Britain still use them. For an example of a stamp tax, look at the duck stamp on most hunting licenses.

The Townshend Acts (1767).
Add taxes to a long list of items shipped from Britain including tea, paper, and painter's supplies.

tax were to be used to defray the costs of colonial defense. The law managed to offend all the wrong people: lawyers, editors, students, and poker players (actually, whist players). Subsequent political administrations, even in our present day, have suggested similarly unpalatable taxes, though the ebb and flow of regular elections has rather dampened this practice.

The Stamp Act produced an eruption. Americans had accepted taxes on overseas trade, imposed ostensibly to regulate and not to raise revenue, but this internal tax, placed directly on individuals, and designed to levy funds, was the last straw. Americans had no representation in Britain's Parliament, and their own colonial legislatures never consented to the tax. This was, in the famous phrase, taxation without representation.

THE UNPLEASANTNESS BEGINS

Protests, demonstrations and riots ensued. Militants shouted slogans and hung official stamp-tax collectors in effigy. Mob violence, a boycott of trade pending repeal of the "black act," and a resolution by nine colonies pledging loyalty but demanding equal rights (the Stamp Act Congress of 1765) were among the heated responses of Britain's so-called subjects.

Now began a cat and mouse game between Britain and the colonies that was to last some ten years, until the battles of Lexington and Concord inaugurated the War for Independence in 1775. In this case, the cat was an overweight Cheshire, and the mouse wore a suit that said "Mighty." If that rabble across the sea doesn't like our Stamp Act, and elects to boycott British goods, said Parliament, we'll cancel that measure, and introduce another (the Townshend Acts of 1767), which shall impose duties on items shipped from England to the colonies. Hundreds of pamphlets arguing the "patriot" cause rolled from American presses in response, decrying this new injustice. Another boycott of British goods undid that act, but tempers remained high: In March, 1770 some Bostonians threw snowballs at a member of the city's despised British garrison. Considering that these missiles didn't even have rocks in the middle, the redcoats clearly overreacted; they fired into the crowd of civilians and killed four. A local lawyer and politician, John Adams (who later made a name for himself as president of the U.S.A.), took on the unpopular task of defending the eight soldiers accused of taking part in what became known as the Boston Massacre. Two years later a British revenue schooner, the *Gaspe,* ran aground near Providence, Rhode Island. A group of anonymous Patriot firebugs seized on this opportunity for a weinie roast by burning the ship to its keel.

In the wake of the *Gaspe* affair, each colony agreed to establish a committee of correspondence to keep in touch with the other colonies on matters of common interest. This vinegary network of leaders established a precedent of cooperation between the states which would later foster the cohesive spirit needed to create a federal government.

DO YOU TAKE SALT WATER
IN YOUR TEA?

Tea induced the contractions that led to the difficult birth of a new nation. The British government passed the Tea Act of 1773, a scheme for cutting American wholesalers out of the channels of tea distribution, and propping up the sales of the faltering East India Company. Lord North and his cabinet erred grievously on the side of avarice; up and down the coast of America the reaction was severe—nowhere more so than in Boston.

On the night of December 16, 1773, a group of row-
dies recruited, we might surmise, from Dartmouth, or
the upper sections of Boston Garden at the end of a
Celtics game, pulled the practical joke of the century.
They dressed up as Indians, boarded three British tea
ships, and dumped 342 chests of tea into the harbor—a
quantity worth about £9,000. Other less famous tea parties followed. Strangely, Britain was neither invited, en-
tertained, nor amused.

The humorless legislature across the ocean didn't find
any humor in this escapade and subsequently passed a
series of repressive laws, which Americans quickly termed
the "Intolerable Acts."
The outraged leaders of Britain's rebellious outposts in
America responded by meeting in Philadelphia in September, 1774 to consider common action. Fifty-five delegates from twelve colonies convened the first Continental
Congress. Some were for peace under imperial rule, others probably didn't care so long as they never again had
to eat bangers and mash, and the rest wished to create

a new empire with tenuous ties to the mother country. The Declaration of Rights that emerged declared that Parliament could "regulate" their affairs in a general sense, but that the colonies had the right to rule and tax themselves.

THE INTOLERABLE ACTS: FIVE WAYS TO MAKE YOURSELF UNPOPULAR WITH COLONISTS

When the British passed the Intolerable Acts, they must have been giving a lot of thought to exactly which measures would offend the most. Here's what they came up with:

1. Close the Port of Boston until Massachusetts reimburses the East India Company for the lost tea.
2. Provide that any British official accused of a crime can be tried elsewhere than in America.
3. Allow British troops to be quartered wherever they are needed, even in private homes (a sure-fire crowd pleaser).
4. Reduce the power of the Massachusetts Colonial Assembly and of local town meetings.
5. Extend the boundary of Canada south of the Great Lakes, checking the westward expansion of the thirteen colonies. Then decree religious toleration for Quebec's Catholics, in order to offend what you know to be the bigoted Protestant sensibilities of the colonists.

"THE SHOT HEARD 'ROUND THE WORLD"

In April 1775, the British ordered General Thomas Gage in Boston to arrest two Massachusetts radical leaders, Sam Adams and John Hancock, and to seize a Patriot arms cache at Concord. Paul Revere, on his famous ride, warned the two patriots about their imminent arrest and so Adams and Hancock escaped. But the British regiment marched to Lexington where they encountered 70 armed American "Minute Men"—a local militia, established by an act of the provincial congress two years earlier, intended to be ready at a minute's notice. When the redcoat officer ordered them to disperse, the Americans moved off, but the settlers did not surrender their muskets. Then, someone in the British ranks fired a shot. The outnumbered Americans returned the volley, but got the worst of the exchange. They retreated from the field of battle, but not before both sides had left bullet holes in surrounding houses that can be seen, under glass, to this day. (Today, a mischievous imagination might wonder, if NASA sent a bunch of cows into orbit, would that be the herd shot round the world?)

The redcoats marched on to Concord where they destroyed some Patriot arms. By now the countryside—every "Middlesex village and farm"—had been alerted. As the British marched back to Boston, the Minute Men took advantage of what today would seem like peculiar rules of engagement: The British had to wear bright red uniforms bearing targets in the form of crossed white straps, and march along in straight lines, while the settlers got to wear earth tones, find good cover, and shoot whenever they pleased. Thus from behind trees and stone walls, the rebels fired lead relentlessly into the retreating column. By the time the British reached safety at their encampment in Boston, 73 had been killed and 174 wounded. A grave, exhilarating chapter in American history had begun.

INDEPENDENCE

King George III (1738–1820), one of the great comic villains of American History.

While violence rapidly pushed Americans toward independence, thousands still refused to support a final break with Britain.

Perhaps a quarter of European-Americans remained loyal to King George III. Most of these merely voiced their opinions or refused to cooperate with the revolutionaries. But several thousand joined the British forces and fought their Patriot countrymen with guns.

At first, not all Patriots favored independence either. Three weeks after the "shot heard 'round the world" at Lexington Green, the Second Continental Congress, more radical than the first, assembled in Philadelphia and established a "continental" army. Here the assembled leaders made what would prove to be an excellent career move for the nation: To lead the new army, they chose a man who'd served superbly in the British military during the French and Indian War. Their first round pick was a surveyor from Fredericksburg, Virginia who, legend says, chopped down a cherry tree and then didn't know enough to put the blame on someone else. In other words, they chose George Washington. At the same time, the delegates also adopted a conciliatory "Olive Branch Petition," which declared American loyalty to George III and asked him to protect them against Parliamentary tyranny. George III responded rather coolly: He hired German mercenaries (Hessians) to put down the Patriot rebellion. Insofar as future income from the New World was concerned, the British king had really made a big mistake.

CRAZY GEORGE AND COMMON SENSE

The king's contempt gave great encouragement to the Patriot radicals, but it was the appearance of a pamphlet called *Common Sense* in early January 1776 that eliminated all doubt. Written by a recently arrived Englishman, Thomas Paine, the fifty-page document called George III "the royal brute," and argued that ·it was foolish for a people with a huge continent in their hands to be pushed around by the reactionary residents of a mere island (one that would someday develop tabloid journalism to unforeseen depths, Paine neglected to add). *Common Sense* was a bugle call for independence. If ever words have changed the world, Paine's did.

JEFFERSON, FRANKLIN, AND ADAMS

On June 7, 1776 Richard Henry Lee of Virginia introduced resolutions in the Continental Congress that called for independence, for foreign alliances to hasten progress toward that goal, and for a confederation of the "united colonies" under some sort of overall frame of government. Congress turned the resolutions over to a committee of three, an intellectual double-play combination that could handle just about anything hit at them: Thomas Jefferson of Virginia, Benjamin Franklin of Pennsylvania, and John Adams of Massachusetts. In this triumvirate lay the intellectual gifts that spawned the Declaration of Independence, a powerful, written statement of aims and beliefs around which the will of a nation-to-be could unite. Jefferson (1743–1826) was born in Virginia. He excelled in a number of pursuits— science, architecture, farming, education, politics, music, and others. A member of the Virginia House of Burgesses, he was made a delegate to the Continental Con-

*"There were quite a few yoks in the original draft,
but they've become lost in subsequent renderings."*

gress in 1776. Two years later he would become the
governor of Virginia, guiding the state through the trou-
bled last years of the American Revolution.

One of Jefferson's partners in this endeavor, Benjamin
Franklin (1706–1790), was likewise a Renaissance man.
Some know of his *Poor Richard's Almanacs,* annual guides
for farmers on weather, astronomical phenomena, and
other matters. Others know him for the classic electrical
experiment involving the key on a kite string in a thun-
derstorm. That incident was historic in a way few people
consider—the first stunt so hare-brained as to require
the warning, "don't try this at home." Beyond these su-
perficial achievements are Franklin's more enduring tri-
umphs. He sailed to England (1757) where he argued
successfully for repeal of the Stamp Act; journeyed to
France (1776) during the Revolutionary War to win the

military support of French officers and French recognition of the United States and he even served early on (1753) as Deputy Postmaster General of the colonies. In those days, the mail didn't just *seem* to be delivered by slow boat; it *was* delivered by slow boat.

BENJAMIN FRANKLIN: A MAN WHO DIDN'T WASTE ANY TIME WATCHING TV

Benjamin Franklin (1706–1790).

From the ages of 12 to 17, he published a newspaper with his brother, then ran an extremely successful printing business. When he was 22, he bought a poorly published newspaper and turned it into a lively and successful journal of news and ideas. By the time he was 26, he had published the first edition of *Poor Richard's Almanack*, the most widely read publication in the colonies for the next 25 years. He founded the American Philosophical Society. He reorganized the American postal system to make it profitable. He founded the University of Pennsylvania, formulated a theory of heat absorption, discovered electrical polarity, measured the Gulf Stream, designed ships, tracked storm paths, invented bifocal lenses, the lighting rod, and the Franklin stove, and studied French, Spanish, Italian, and Latin in his spare time. He co-authored the Declaration of Independence, and then finally, at the age of 81, even though he was so crippled by gout that he couldn't stand up, he attended the Constitutional Convention, making significant contributions to the final document. He was also a devoted husband (despite a reputation as a ladies' man) and the doting father of ten children.

John Adams (1735–1826).

A third titan of the era who aided the drafting of the Declaration of Independence was John Adams (1735–1826) of Massachusetts. He was an exceedingly talented political thinker who supported the creation of the Continental army, and from 1778 to 1788 lived largely abroad, where he took on a series of diplomatic assignments on behalf of the U.S. In 1796 he would become the second president of the United States.

THE DECLARATION OF INDEPENDENCE

Working together, these three figures who'd play such essential roles in the early years of nationhood sat down to plan the first punch in the imperial gut. Jefferson wrote the draft of a statement justifying and explaining independence; the other two edited it. The document they composed passed Congress on July 4, 1776.

The Declaration of Independence was at once an indictment of British policy and a statement of the new nation's underlying principles. It listed scores of British "abuses and usurpations," many exaggerated, some even false, in order to justify separation. Like the good PR men who toil in politics today, the three authors recognized the importance of public perception. But the manifesto announced a rebellious people's guiding philosophies to a world full of inbred monarchies.

This remarkable document drew on sophisticated notions of human rights that were rooted in the period of "Enlightenment" in eighteenth-century Europe. The Declaration proclaimed that all men were "created equal" and were endowed by "their Creator with certain unalienable rights" including "Life, Liberty, and the pursuit of Happiness." Governments, it continued, were "instituted among men" to "secure these rights" and these governments "derived their just powers from the consent of the governed."

Such assertions aren't very startling today, and we know that Jefferson and his colleagues weren't thinking of women, of blacks, or of other races when they wrote. But in 1776 the claims of the Declaration were a bold attack on privilege and tyranny that would inspire later independence movements around the globe.

"We hold these truths to be self-serving . . . make that self-evident."

REVOLUTION AND WAR

The Declaration was fighting words. On paper, the Americans, pitted against a world power, were clearly outclassed. On the other hand, Britain was 3,000 miles away from the battlefields and would find it difficult and expensive to bring its power to bear on the rebels. America, moreover, had likely allies in France and Spain, countries that, while possessed of finer cuisines than England, still smarted from the losses they sustained in the French and Indian wars.

THE EARLY CAMPAIGNS

The opening campaigns of the revolutionary war were not entirely successful for the Americans. Soon after

Lexington and Concord, General Thomas Gage in Boston, the same man who masterminded the debacle at Lexington and Concord, found himself facing American troops dug in atop Breed's Hill, a rise that overlooked the city. From there, the Americans could rain artillery fire directly into his camp. (Modern tourists can visit the famous monument to the battle at Boston's "Bunker Hill" but these visitors generally don't learn until they get there that this obelisk was constructed on the wrong high ground: Patriots abandoned Bunker Hill for a different position on nearby Breed's Hill shortly before the British attacked.) Although Gage finally evicted the Americans, he lost about one-third of his men—a hammer blow. He subsequently resigned. Soon after, however, Washington arrived to take command of the Continental army, and Gage concluded he could no longer hold the city. In March 1776 the British army departed by sea for Halifax.

Meanwhile, the Americans under Generals Richard Montgomery and Benedict Arnold effected a modest plan to capture Canada, an adventure that left Montgomery dead and the British still in control. Arnold, known to every schoolchild as the personification of deceit and treachery, was a brave and effective general, severely wounded twice, praised by Congress, and promoted by Washington. (But of course, there was that unpleasantness at West Point, which he tried—unsuccessfully—to betray to the British.) In the South, Americans fared better, destroying an army of Loyalists in North Carolina and preventing the British from capturing Charleston. Not bad for an expansion team.

In 1776–77 the Americans suffered a series of defeats in the middle states. In August 1776, General William Howe trounced Washington at the Battle of Long Island, and chased the father of our country all the way to White Plains. Probably caught up with him during rush hour on New York City's Cross-Bronx Expressway. Washington was really back-pedaling now, retreating across New Jersey to Pennsylvania. But he turned his fortunes around that Christmas with a successful surprise attack on Britain's Hessian mercenaries at Trenton. He may not have actually stood up in the front of the boat as the famous painting suggests, but he did cross the Delaware (at a town now called Washington's Crossing) and captured a thousand German mercenaries.

This hardly requires a caption. Washington's famous (and rather unlikely) pose, crossing the Delaware.

The British planned a knockout blow for the summer of 1777 and almost succeeded. In July, Howe moved his 15,000 troops by sea from New York and prepared to march on Philadelphia. Washington rushed to stop him, but was beaten at Brandywine Creek. On September 19, Congress fled Philadelphia. That winter, often seen as the nadir of American fortunes, Washington took his army into winter quarters at Valley Forge, not far from the British-occupied City of Brotherly Love. The American troops suffered severely from cold and hunger, mostly due to the quartermasters' incompetence and bad planning.

1777: GOOD YEAR FOR THE AMERICANS, BUMMER FOR THE BRITS

Fortunately for the Americans, the other major British campaign of 1777 failed miserably, and so began the slow process of British collapse. In June, while General Howe was pursuing Washington from pillar to bedpost, a force of 7,000 British, German, Canadian, and Indian fighters led by General John Burgoyne set out from Canada for parts south. Burgoyne aimed to move along the

---

DRAMATIC TIMES FOR JOHN BURGOYNE

Burgoyne is one of those generals who, like the 1951 Dodgers, is remembered best for a big loss. But Burgoyne, like the Dodgers, won a few before being humiliated in the end. In Burgoyne's case, he began the invasion of the colonies with big victories at Ticonderoga, for which he was made a lieutenant-general, and at Fort Edward. Part of his problem at Saratoga was that William Howe, who was supposed to meet him, never received his instructions—the Americans had cleverly cut his communications with Canada. Everyone agrees today that the defeat was not his fault at all. Even though Burgoyne lost at Saratoga to a clearly superior force, the British, unsympathetic, fired him anyway. Fortunately, he had another career: He was a highly successful playwright, whose first play, *The Maid of the Oaks*, was produced by David Garrick in 1775. His comedy, *The Heiress*, was a huge success in England and, translated into several foreign languages, a success abroad as well. He left two volumes of plays and poems when he died in 1792.

Hudson to New York, cutting the colonies in two. For a time the British made headway but each day of advance stretched thin their lines of supply. Eventually, hastily gathered American troops ground down "gentleman Johnny's" force as it marched, and ultimately surrounded the redcoats at Saratoga. On October 17, as Washington's beleaguered army established a winter camp at Valley Forge, Burgoyne accepted the inevitable and surrendered his remaining 5,700 men and all his equipment to the American leader Horatio Gates. Burgoyne's war was over. He went back to England where he resumed his alternate career as a dramatist.

TURNING POINT: THE ALLIANCE WITH FRANCE

Saratoga was the turning point. The victory charged up American morale by proving that the sons of liberty could beat the best troops the mother country could muster. Even more important, this triumph of sheer will over professionalism brought France into the war as an American ally.

The French had been unofficially helping America with money and arms for some time before the episode at Saratoga. This support stemmed in part from support for "freedom," a stylish cause among France's intellectuals, professionals, and the "enlightened" nobility, who viewed Americans as "natural" men living in some Edenic paradise and battling a cruel tyrant. These were the spiritual ancestors of the French intellectuals who today idolize the American actors Jerry Lewis and Mickey Rourke. Their questionable taste in pop icons aside, in the old days we needed all the friends we could get.

France formally recognized American independence and negotiated a treaty of alliance with the new United States. France was now in the war and its financial and military aid would prove invaluable. In mid-1779 Spain also declared war on Britain, though the conservative Spanish government remained suspicious of the American rebels, and offered the equivalent of a limp handshake on the deal.

THE ARTICLES OF CONFEDERATION

Congress had proposed a more permanent political structure than the Second Continental Congress for the "united colonies," and in July 1776 John Dickinson, "Penman of the Revolution," already influential and widely known for his anti-Townshend Acts "Letters of a Farmer in Pennsylvania," presented a plan that became the basis of a protracted debate.

It is not surprising, given colonial jealousies, that the new "Articles of Confederation" established a weak central government. This government would decide disputes between the states and conduct affairs with foreign nations for them all. But the central government would share with the states the power to coin money and would need the approval of nine states to adopt treaties, declare war, raise troops, or borrow funds. It couldn't levy taxes; the states had to fund the federal authorities and, no surprise, they seldom volunteered to do so. The new federal government lacked a separate executive branch and it had no machinery to enforce its will on the states. Still, it took until 1781 for the Articles to be adopted, largely because several states refused to vote favorably until all the states had surrendered their land claims in the West to the new central authority. By 1781, the United States had a legal central government, but the whole did not yet add up to more than the sum of its parts. Instead of a nation, the U.S. was a voluntary league of sovereign mini-nations.

VICTORY

Meanwhile the fighting went on. In the late spring of 1778 Washington's army, after surviving an exhausting winter with inadequate clothing, food, and shelter, came out of quarters at Valley Forge. The troops were depleted in numbers but strengthened in discipline and training. By this time, Sir Henry Clinton, who had succeeded Howe as chief of the British command, had evacuated Philadelphia with the intention of concentrating his force in New York. On June 28, the Americans tried to prevent these troops from returning to New York. The ensuing Battle of Monmouth was a draw and the British army escaped.

The British and their Indian allies (it was a well-established tradition among colonial powers to stop slaughtering the Indians just long enough to use them in temporary alliances against more compelling opponents) attacked American settlements on the Pennsylvania and New York frontiers. The following year, American forces under George Rogers Clark and John Sullivan defeated the British and the Iroquois in several battles in the trans-Appalachian region, bringing relative peace to the frontier and allowing American farmers and traders to pour across the mountains and establish flourishing communities in what would later become Kentucky and Tennessee, the latter being the present-day home of Nashville and Dollywood. This begs one of those great what-if questions that historians seem to miss, namely would we as a nation have had country & western music without these victories? And if not, would there have been an Elvis?

Despite the Saratoga victory, 1780 was in some ways the low point of the war for the Americans. After five years of fighting, weariness had set in. Many young men were willing to fight the British, but deserted after a few months of summer campaigning. In May, Washington's troops, encamped at Morristown, New Jersey, mutinied over sparse rations and serious arrears in pay. Fortunately for American independence, Pennsylvania troops quelled the mutiny, but this was a close shave. In January 1781, the Pennsylvania troops themselves mutinied, and had to be bought off.

IF ONLY THEY'D THOUGHT OF JUNK BONDS . . .

During the revolutionary war, just as today, Americans did not want to pay taxes, even for independence, and Congress was forced to borrow money at high interest rates, pay for supplies with IOUs, and ultimately resort to massive issues of paper money, called "Continentals." The paper money quickly plummeted in value and much of the debt went into default. Sound familiar? Ironically, today the "Continental" bills can fetch good money from numismatists and other collectors.

CORNWALLIS DOES A HEADSTAND

In the perilous year of 1781, when morale in the Continental army began to fracture like thin ice, the rebels were finally blessed with an end to the fighting. The crucial battle came at Yorktown, Virginia, where the British general, Charles Cornwallis, was hemmed in on a narrow peninsula by American and French forces. He could count on reinforcement and resupply by General Sir Henry Clinton in New York only as long as the British navy controlled the seas. But the Royal Navy let him down. In September the French fleet forced the British to withdraw their ships to New York, cutting Cornwallis's lifeline. Slowly Franco-American military pressure grew. On October 16 Cornwallis tried and failed to break out of the trap. On October 18 he surrendered his entire force of 8,000 men. As the redcoats marched out of their stockade to stack their arms, their band played "The World Turned Upside Down."

The defeat at Yorktown convinced most Britons that the war was hopeless. In March, 1782 the ministry of Lord North resigned and a more conciliatory cabinet took its place.

PEACE

In June, 1782 peace talks opened in Paris between Richard Oswald for Britain and John Jay, John Adams, and Benjamin Franklin for the United States. The final settlement conceded American independence within fuzzy and complicated boundaries in the north and south, and at the Mississippi to the west. Hostilities would cease and all British forces still on American soil would leave "with all convenient speed." Americans would retain certain fishing rights in Newfoundland and Nova Scotia waters, but the American government would "earnestly recommend" that the state legislatures fully restore the rights and property of loyalists and urge repayment of long overdue debts to British creditors. (This would have the same impact as a polite request for scofflaws to pay their parking tickets.)

On April 15, 1783 Congress ratified the Treaty of Paris. Ten days later, 7,000 loyalists sailed from New York, which was still in British hands, to take up new lives in Britain, Canada, or other British colonies. Seven months after that the last British troops left New York, and Washington said farewell to his officers in New York City.

The war was over. The former English colonies were now an independent nation with all the opportunities, hopes, and hazards that the word freedom implies, and a chance to develop glitzy popular culture that would eventually influence the world.

SUMMARY

⏱ Britain wanted the colonies for its own purposes—to make them an integral part of the Empire, from which the British could profit.

⏱ The cost of an imperial defense was overwhelming—and the British felt the Americans should pay for it with taxes.

⏱ The colonies organized and went to war to prevent the British from taxing them without their permission, or exploiting the wealth of the new continent without sharing it with the people who lived there.

⏱ Though the initial catalyst for the Declaration of Independence was economic, the document turned out to be a bold and inspiring attack on privilege and tyranny. The Declaration heralded a new form of government that embodied many of the liberating ideals of the European Enlightenment of the eighteenth century (also called the Age of Reason).

CHAPTER 3

THE CONSTITUTION
AND THE PARTY SYSTEM

YOU MUST REMEMBER THIS

The Articles of Confederation were a failed compromise: they'd created a central government all right—but it was a government with no power to govern. This couldn't last. The country needed something remarkable to survive, and something remarkable is exactly what it got: the Constitution and the Bill of Rights.

IMPORTANT EVENTS

★ The Land Ordinance of 1785
★ The Northwest Ordinance, 1787
★ The Constitutional Convention, 1787
★ Ratification of the Constitution, 1788
★ George Washington elected President, 1789
★ French Revolution, 1789
★ John Adams elected President, 1796
★ The Alien and Sedition Acts, 1798
★ Thomas Jefferson elected President, 1800

As the American Revolution ended, peace and independence from Britain were welcomed with pealing church bells, bonfires, and parades. But not so fast, folks: Despite the initial jollity, the next five years, often called "the Critical Period," turned out to be a time of crisis and difficult readjustment. This tumultuous era culminated in the Constitutional Convention of 1787. The outcome of that summer-long meeting in Philadelphia would be the famous document whose supple, articulate provisions have sustained the U.S. through difficulties that the founding fathers could never have imagined.

WHO'S WHO ☞

Do These Names Ring a Bell?

🖎 **George Washington** (1732–1799).
Soldier, statesman, first president of the United States (1788–96).

🖎 **Alexander Hamilton** (1757–1804).
Aide to Washington, member of Continental Congress, first secretary of the Treasury.

🖎 **Edmund Randolph** (1753–1813).
Member of Constitutional Convention, governor of Virginia, Attorney General, and secretary of state.

🖎 **John Jay** (1745–1829).
Jurist and statesman, member of Continental Congress, ambassador to Spain, secretary of state, chief justice of the Supreme Court

WHO'S
H
O
☞

(*continued*)

(1789–95), governor of New York (1795–1801).

🕮 **Thomas Jefferson** (1743–1826).
Third president of the United States, drafter of the Declaration of Independence, secretary of state under Washington, vice-president in 1797, and president in 1801.

🕮 **John Adams** (1735–1826).
Second president of the United States, delegate to Continental Congress. Proposed Washington as president, vice-president under Washington 1788–96, and president 1796–1800.

🕮 **Aaron Burr** (1756–1863).
U.S. senator and vice-president 1800–1804. Tied with Jefferson in 1800 in vote for president, but was defeated in the House of Representatives. Mortally wounded Alexander Hamilton in a duel in 1804.

HARD TIMES AND WAR BUCKS

Battling the Brits from 1775 to 1781 cost plenty. War is always lucrative for some. The paper money issued by Congress and cash from both the French and British armies meant higher prices for farmers and merchants.

This was good for them. Artisans, protected against British manufacturers, had prospered. But after the binge, there's always the hangover; peace brought hard times. British goods flooded into the United States and consumers snapped them up like Japanese TV sets. This drained gold and silver from the country, deflated prices, and squeezed debtors severely. To make matters worse, the British excluded American shippers—now foreigners—from the formerly lucrative trade with British possessions in the West Indies and elsewhere. Farming, overseas trade, and manufacturing were all, to put it as generously as possible, in the dumper. More than a few Americans wondered if being independent of Britain was such a good idea after all!

AND YOU THOUGHT REAGAN LEFT THE ECONOMY IN SHAMBLES

Government debts were also a problem—an even bigger problem than they are today, hard though that may be to believe. While a few states had taxed their citizens after 1783 to pay wartime debts, most of the former colonies had let their IOUs go into default. Congress too had failed to pay its domestic creditors and had not been able to pay back money borrowed from the French and Dutch. The finances of the new nation were a mess, and our international credit rating was a null set.

Compounding the woes of struggling leaders, citizens from Maine to Georgia were unhappy with the postwar regime, and demanded change. In some states, debtors and farmers induced legislatures to issue new paper money to raise prices and stimulate business. This ham-handed solution failed, which hasn't stopped people from trying it on a regular basis ever since.

BEHIND THE SCENES

Little-Known Players and Unsung Heroes

People, few of them white males, who don't always make it into the history books.

Daniel Shays (1747–1825).
Leader of a rebellion by Massachusetts farmers demanding a stop to the foreclosures on farms and the printing of more paper money by the state. The rebellion was a significant impetus to the establishment of stronger central government.

Hector St. Jean de Crèvecoeur (1735–1813).
A French farmer and naturalist who emigrated to America. His most famous work, *Letters From An American Farmer*, was a series of essays presenting an insightful and sympathetic portrait of life in America.

Hannah Adams (1755–1831).
The first American woman to make a living by writing. Author of *A Summary History of New England* (1799).

Benjamin Banneker (1731–1806).
A black man who taught himself mathematics and astronomy, accurately predicted a solar eclipse, and was appointed to plan the new city of Washington.

Rhode Island was one of the states that issued its own paper money. When the value of the notes depreciated, merchants and creditors refused to accept them in payment for goods, though they were required to do so by law. The joke went around that debtors flush with Rhode Island "legal tenders," pursued their creditors unceasingly, and paid them without mercy.

Artisans and manufacturers also sought relief, and states passed tariff laws to exclude foreign-made goods. Merchants responded by importing goods from abroad via adjacent states. A rat's nest of tariffs began to accumulate, making it look as if the United States would disintegrate into a rabble of mini-nations waging perpetual trade war.

WEAK ECONOMY AND WEAKER GOVERNMENT: A BAD COMBINATION

Many of the postwar economic difficulties could be blamed on the weak central government established under the Articles of Confederation. Congress couldn't pay its debts because it couldn't tax. It couldn't even pay the veterans who had fought for independence!

Without the power to regulate interstate or foreign commerce, the national government could neither fend off foreign competition in the American market nor strong-arm European governments to open their markets to U.S. goods. In short, neither the British nor anyone else much feared the economic power of this motley new nation.

Britain's tough policies in trade were due in part to sour grapes; it would be wrong, however, to assume that they ruefully anticipated the time when their most vital export to this side of the Atlantic would be the TV show "Masterpiece Theatre," for that, of course, came later.

The Americans had failed to abide by the peace treaty's provision for the restitution of loyalist property. Here too the weak Articles of Confederation could be blamed. Congress recommended that the states compensate colonists who'd been loyal to Britain, oddly named the loyalists, but the states didn't feel like it. So they didn't. In retaliation, the British refused to abandon their military posts on American soil as promised, and the lingering British presence in the Northwest put a damper on the high spirits of American fur traders in that region.

If Britain was condescending to the new nation, Spain was downright contemptuous. Under the 1783 peace treaty, Spain retained Louisiana and the vital port of New Orleans. By this time thousands of pioneer farmers lived on the "Western Waters" and used the Mississippi and its tributaries to ship their surplus goods to market. However, goods sent down the Father of Waters by raft or keel boat had to be transshipped at New Orleans for ocean-going ships, and this required that Spain grant the farmers the "right of deposit" at the city's wharves. The Spaniards would not grant Americans this privilege. Though the birthplace of the bullfight was a nation in decline, it could still stick it to the U.S. of A. Meanwhile, Western farmers were deprived of a vital outlet for their furs, timber, pork, and grain.

Businessmen of the time had ample reason to wish for a stronger central power, and collectively agitated for change. Furthermore, these "interest groups" were not the only ones to deplore the weakness of the Articles government. Patriots—or nationalists—were disgruntled too. Many patriots had been soldiers and officers during the war, and were now appalled by the weak pseudonation that victory over King George had created. It was hard for such stout souls not to feel contempt for Congress, a body that often couldn't even raise a quorum, never mind a tax. If Ross Perot had been alive to head

these sons of liberty, the consequences for that day's
tassle-shoed bandits of the Beltway would have been terri-
ble to behold.

THE NORTHWEST

Despite the new nation's troubles, the national government that functioned under the Articles of Confederation could claim two significant achievements, both
related to the western frontier.

NEW TOWNS AND SLAVE-FREE STATES

Congress had inherited all former crown lands and
lands claimed by the states in the trans-Appalachian region. The Land Ordinance of 1785 required a survey to
eliminate the conflicting land claims that had caused
such confusion during the colonial period. The surveyed
lands would be laid out in townships, expediting the
equitable settlement of new territories. There would be
a federal-aid-to-education plan as part of the whole: One
lot in each township would be reserved for support of a
school. If the masterminds of expansion had really been
on the ball, they'd have reserved a strip behind the designated landfill zones where all the fast food joints would
have to huddle together for warmth.

The second great measure for the West, the Northwest
Ordinance of 1787, established a system of government
for western regions located north of the Ohio River.
Under the terms of this decree, the region initially would
be administered by a governor and by judges whom Congress would appoint. When the territory had reached a
population that included 5,000 free adult males, it would
elect a legislature with limited powers. Ultimately, from
three to five states with at least 60,000 persons each

might be carved from the region. These states would be admitted "on an equal footing with the original states in all respects whatsoever." A final controversial provision excluded slavery forever from such settled areas. Remember that one for when we get to the Civil War.

WE THE PEOPLE

These breakthrough land laws were nice, but it was clear to everyone that the American government, such as it was, was utterly inadequate as a player on the international scene, and was not even equipped to hold together the 13 states at home. Before long a major effort was underway to alter or supersede the Articles to provide the new nation with a more effective central government.

The result, to the surprise of everyone involved, was the U.S. Constitution.

HOT TIME IN PHILLY

The drive culminated in a call by Congress for a convention to meet in Philadelphia in May 1787 to "render the constitution of the federal government adequate to the exigencies of the Union."

Fifty-five sweaty men convened in Philadelphia. It was a sweltering summer, and in those days real men wore wigs. Had the issue been put to a vote, Benjamin Franklin would have been required to invent air conditioning by unanimous consent. Those present were hardly a representative cross section of the American people. There were no women, no blacks, no small farmers, no artisans. Most delegates were lawyers while the rest were planters, merchants, doctors, and college professors. They were generally wealthy and some were speculators in the unpaid Congressional debt, and so bear the honor of being among the first inside traders in American history. It was a remarkable assemblage of talent and status. Everyone would have been in the Social Register—if there had been one. Among the outstanding national leaders pres-

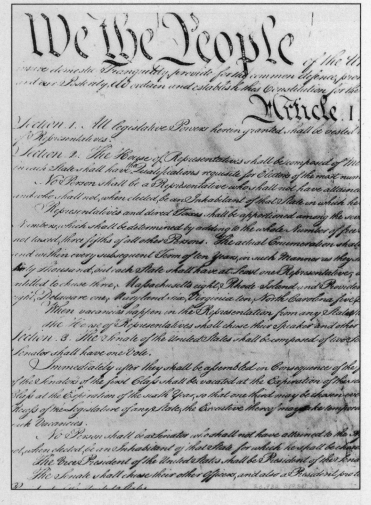

The Constitution.

ent were George Washington, Benjamin Franklin, James Madison of Virginia, and Alexander Hamilton of New York. Surprise! The document they wrote established a government of the elite.

Hamilton had begun his career of public service as

THE GAME OF THE NAME

As you well know by now, the Constitutional Convention had plenty of big names—Washington, Franklin, Jefferson, Madison, Hamilton—and if you are situated in the U.S. and happen not to be near a city, a town, or maybe a bridge bearing one of these names, then you're probably in Alaska or Hawaii. Other eighteenth-century celebs also attended: William Paterson, later the governor of New Jersey, for whom Paterson, New Jersey is named; Gouverneur Morris, a politician and large landowner in New York, whose name is immortalized in, among other New York locales, the Morrisania section of the Bronx; and Elbridge Gerry, who became the governor of Massachusetts and vice-president of the U.S. under Madison. Gerry's name is forever attached to the carving up of electoral districts for political gain, a practice known as "gerrymandering."

This 1812 engraving by Elkanah Tisdale from the Boston Weekly Messenger *depicts Governor Elbridge Gerry's redefinition of the state's voting districts as "THE GERRY-MANDER!" so called because the newly delineated district of Marblehead appeared on the map in the shape of a giant salamander.*

secretary to George Washington during the Revolutionary War. As we shall see, he later founded the Federalist Party, espoused close relations with Britain, and voiced opposition to the French Revolution, showing his uneasiness with the notion of real rule by the great unwashed masses—that is, "we the people." Despite his reactionary views, he would eventually be tapped to manage the U.S. Treasury, which he did with foresight and skill.

These men had no desire to encourage wealth redistribution or "mob rule"—code words for helping the poor, and for government by the people. "Checks and balances" between the legislative, judicial, and executive branches were intended as much to block temporary popular enthusiasms as to prevent tyranny. The framers were careful to do nothing that might undercut slavery—they couldn't afford to offend the populous states of the South and many of them were slave holders themselves. Yet the delegates also cherished freedom and the document would contain "democratic" features along with "aristocratic" ones.

BIG STATES, SMALL STATES, AND TAXATION WITH REPRESENTATION

On May 29 Edmund Randolph proposed what came to be called the Virginia Plan. This would be a completely new design for government, not merely a revision of the Articles. It would establish a two-house legislature in which the states would be represented in proportion to their population, with the lower house elected by "the people" and the upper house chosen by the lower house. The executive (our version of the monarch in Europe) in this new government would also be elected by the legislature as would the judges of a new set of federal courts.

The Virginia Plan favored the large states over the small ones. So the latter group countered with the New

Jersey Plan. First, the Articles would merely be revised, not superseded, by new ones. Each state would have equal representation in Congress and that body would have enhanced powers to tax and regulate foreign and domestic commerce. Congress would also name an executive branch consisting of more than one man.

In the end, the delegates decided to replace the Articles of Confederation with a new constitution, but they compromised on representation. The new Congress would have two houses: the Senate, with an equal number of representatives from each state, and the House of Representatives, whose number of representatives per state would be based on population. For the purpose of establishing the states' respective populations, the convention accepted what now seems a rather bizarre compromise on valuing the states' populations of slaves: each person in "servitude" (the document avoided the word "slave" so as not to offend the delicate ears of that

---

WHAT THE NEW NATIONAL GOVERNMENT COULD DO THAT THE CONTINENTAL CONGRESS BEFORE IT COULD NOT: A TOP TEN LIST

1. Borrow money and impose taxes and duties
2. Regulate foreign and interstate commerce
3. Make uniform naturalization and bankruptcy laws
4. Coin money
5. Establish uniform weights and measures
6. Provide for a postal service
7. Grant patents and copyrights
8. Create an army and a navy
9. Declare war
10. Make treaties with foreign powers

portion of the public that was against the institution) would count as three-fifths of a man.

Other provisions adopted included a one-man executive office (the president) who'd be elected by an electoral college and would hold a veto over congressional legislation that could be overridden by a two-thirds vote. A federal judiciary was also created, capped by a Supreme Court, the members of which would be nominated by the president and confirmed by the Senate. Federal judges would serve for life and the federal courts would handle questions of federal law and disputes between the states. Unspecified, but understood, was the Supreme Court's power to review congressional legislation deemed to violate the Constitution.

To encourage commercial and legal uniformity the Constitution declared that each state should give "full faith and credit" to the judicial proceedings of every other state and that each state should permit the extradition of escaped criminals to the locale where the crime had been committed. Whether the Founding Fathers considered the possibility of residents of, say, Massachusetts buying clothes from out-of-state mail order firms, and dodging state sales tax thereby, is not recorded.

After a committee had revised and rearranged the clauses the document went to the whole convention for approval. Congress accepted the document on September 28 and transmitted it to the states for ratification by special conventions. It was agreed that when nine states had ratified the Constitution, it would go into effect. Considering that it only took a couple of months to create a federal government from scratch, one wonders whether the congressmen of today, who seem to have graduate degrees in partisan squabbling and self-preservation, would benefit from a lunch hour stroll down to the National Archives, where the original Constitution itself can be reread without charge.

RATIFICATION: 13 FOR 13,
EVEN THOUGH IT WAS A BIT DICEY
AT TIMES

People in states like Virginia, New York, North Carolina, and Rhode Island, who were doing fine under the old Articles, thank you very much, saw little advantage in the new union. These were called anti-federalists (opponents of the new "federal" system). Weaker states, or ones that had a hard time going it alone, tended to favor the Constitution. Among such federalists states were New Jersey, Maryland, Georgia, and Connecticut.

In the federalist states, ratification occurred almost without a hitch. But where opinion was negative or divided,

SMALL STATE WITH AN ATTITUDE:
HOW PESKY RHODE ISLAND ALMOST
BECAME AN INDEPENDENT COUNTRY

The Constitutional Convention was actually attended by only 12 states. Rhode Island's leaders, convinced by farmers that a stronger federal government would only mean higher taxes for all, decided to stay home. All their fears were realized when they read the document that emerged. When it came time to ratify, Rhode Island balked again, even going so far as to have their senate pass a bill severing commercial relations with the other united states. Having thus established their independence, Rhode Islanders ultimately decided they *could* ratify the Constitution, though their senate waited until May, 1790 to do so—after every other state had already signed on. Even then, the state senate came within 2 votes of not joining, which would, among other consequences, have denied Boston's professional baseball team access to a lively farm club: the Pawtucket Red Sox or "Paw Sox," as they're affectionately known.

fierce debates raged. In several states the question of protecting personal liberties against the powers of the new federal government became an important issue. Most states had a bill of rights in their own constitutions limiting state powers over citizens, but the authority of the federal government was not similarly restricted in the new document. Defenders of freedom insisted that they would not vote for the Constitution unless they were assured that it would be quickly amended to include such restrictions.

New Hampshire, the ninth state to approve the Constitution, ratified in June 1788. Officially the Constitution was in effect. New York and Virginia soon acquiesced.

THE BILL OF RIGHTS . . . .

Here's the abbreviated list of topics covered. Memorize them and impress your friends:

1. Freedom of press, speech, assembly and religion
2. The right to bear arms (a favorite of the NRA)
3. The government shall keep its soldiers out of citizens' homes
4. Restrictions on Searches and Seizures
5. Due process of law, e.g. no double jeopardy (i.e. you can't be tried twice for the same crime . . . this item no relation to the game show) no self incrimination, and no punishment without a legal process.
6. Trial by jury for criminal cases
7. Trial by jury for civil cases
8. Cruel and unusual punishment a must (just kidding; actually, aside from forcing people to watch game shows, it's prohibited)
9. The specification of these rights doesn't preclude other rights
10. The reserve clause: Rights not given to the U.S. are reserved to the states or the people

North Carolina approved in November, but rebellious little Rhode Island did not join until May 1790. In the fall of 1789 Congress passed the Bill of Rights, which contained the first ten amendments to the Constitution.

THE ELECTORAL COLLEGE ELECTS ITS FIRST PRESIDENT

In January 1789, the members of the presidential electoral college, chosen either by the state legislatures or directly by qualified voters—qualified in those days meaning white and male, often with property, who went to the right church on Sunday, in case you were wondering—met and cast their ballots unanimously for George Washington with John Adams as his vice-president. Congress met for the first time in New York City, the temporary national capital, in March. On April 30 George Washington recited the oath of office on the balcony of Federal Hall in lower Manhattan and then delivered his inaugural address to Congress in the Senate chamber.

THE "FIRST PARTY" SYSTEM

Modern democratic governments need political parties to conceive programs and policies and to mobilize voters and legislatures to enact these programs into law. Many of the political leaders during the early years of constitutional government deplored parties, but such organizations became necessary in order to carry out expeditiously and, alas, not so expeditiously, the work of government. In the course of confronting an array of fresh challenges during the 1790s, the first system of American party government was born.

THE EARLIEST LEGISLATION

Among the earliest acts of Congress was the creation of four executive departments: State, Treasury, War, and the Post Office. Thomas Jefferson and Alexander Hamilton were made the Secretaries of State and Treasury. Soon after, in the Federal Judiciary Act of 1789, Congress specified a chief justice and five associates for the Supreme Court, and established a system of district and circuit federal courts.

Another important early measure was the Tariff Act of 1789 which levied a small tax on a long list of imports, primarily for the purpose of finally providing a revenue source for the federal government, which forestalled such unlikely alternatives as "the mother of all bake sales." We may presume that if President Washington had been challenged on this measure, the man who allegedly chopped the cherry tree would've replied that he'd merely promised "no new axes," and had been misheard.

THE FATHER OF OUR COUNTRY AS A YOUNG MAN.

THE FATHER OF OUR COUNTRY AS A SEASONED ELDER.

T. HAGGERTY

THE HAMILTONIAN PROGRAM

In domestic affairs, President George Washington would look for guidance primarily to Alexander Hamilton, a brilliant young New Yorker born in the West Indies. Hamilton had attended the Constitutional Convention where he had favored a much stronger central government than what was finally established. When asked by Washington to head the new Treasury Department, the young lawyer (he was 32 at the time) saw his chance to further centralize political power and at the same time remake America into an urban-commercial nation, one replete with failed Savings and Loans, farm foreclosures, trillions in debt, and despite such ills, the most widely admired economy on the planet. Whether or not we like the result, Hamilton took the opportunity, and we live with the consequences.

ADDING TO THE FEDERAL DEBT

Hamilton's Report on the Public Credit of January 1790 outlined a plan for paying the overdue debts of the Union and restoring faith in the country's securities by exchanging them for new ones that would pay both principal and interest in gold. It also recommended taking over the unpaid obligations of the states, which would add to the total federal debt, but also build support for the new federal government among the creditors of individual states.

WHY WASHINGTON, D.C. IS THE NATION'S CAPITAL

The "funding" process would clearly improve the public credit and centralize power. But funding would also add to the country's money supply, for the new securities would circulate like money. It was believed that an increased supply of money would in turn reverse the price drops that had occurred since the end of the war and thus stimulate the production of more goods that could be sold at these higher prices.

James Madison (1751–1836).

In Congress, opponents of Hamilton's funding program, like James Madison, said the plan favored speculators to the disadvantage of the original holders of state and federal securities. Many opponents were Southerners who claimed that the assumption of states' debts benefited the North and made the federal government too powerful. Faced with defeat, Hamilton had an idea. He offered Madison and the other Southern leaders a bribe: In exchange for an agreement to locate the nation's permanent capital on the Potomac River, they would in turn support assumption. Suddenly "principles" yielded. The Southern congressmen voted yea, the funding measure passed, and the future profitability of the Washington-New York air shuttle was assured. Public credit soared, and the congressional practice of bargaining for votes became an unwritten codicil to Article I of the Constitution.

THE BANK OF THE UNITED STATES

A year after his first report came out, Hamilton submitted a second, the Report on a National Bank, in which he envisioned a nation where manufacturing would take equal place with agriculture through active government participation. The process would be expedited by a federally chartered Bank of the United States, partially owned by the government, that would make loans available to entrepreneurs. The bank's capital, in part, would come from the federally funded national debt. The new bank would issue paper money, backed by its capital, and these notes could be lent to capitalists to start new businesses or expand old ones. The bank would also lend money to the government, transfer government funds from place to place as needed, and help collect federal duties. Two centuries later, the former Soviet Union is taking its own first steps down the same primrose path.

Again there were loud objections. Jefferson and his friends in Congress believed that the Constitution nowhere authorized a national bank and feared any further extension of federal power. Washington himself was uncertain of the bank's legality and before signing the bill incorporating Hamilton's ideas, asked his two leading cabinet officers to submit opinions on the measure's constitutionality. Jefferson noted that creating a bank was not among the powers specifically delegated to Congress. His "strict construction" views were rejected by Hamilton. The power to incorporate a bank was "implied" by the power to collect taxes and regulate trade. His opinion, a "loose construction" view of the Constitution, proved convincing to Washington and he signed the bill establishing the Bank of the United States.

THE JEFFERSONIANS

Hamilton's policies were popular in the nation's coastal regions, the flourishing ports where merchants, shopkeepers, skilled artisans, shipbuilders, and others connected with commerce and manufacture supported them. Farmers close to these towns who stood to profit directly from new markets overseas and in the growing cities also favored them. But interior farmers and planters—often debtors—saw little benefit to themselves in it. These adversaries were concentrated in the South and West.

HAMILTON VS. JEFFERSON

But more than material interest separated the two groups. According to Jefferson, manufacturers encouraged urbanization and "great cities." Such places were like sores on the human body and their inhabitants were "rabble." Let "our workshops remain abroad" and let Americans concentrate on growing crops, he said. Unlike city "artificers," farmers who owned their own land could be counted on to support honest "republican" government, for their property gave them independence. They accused Hamilton and his friends of favoring monarchy. Hamilton's foes, Jefferson especially, considered themselves "republicans" at the very least, if not democrats in the modern sense of the term. Human nature, they insisted, was inherently good and, unlike their opponents who believed people were capable of any wickedness and easily swayed by demagogues, they

Monticello, Jefferson's country cottage.

trusted majorities (if the majorities were composed of farmers, that is). Though Hamilton graces the $10 bill while Jefferson makes do with the suspect $2 bill (also the nickel), the currency of the latter's views is higher among "rabble" Americans wherever they might live.

FEDERALISTS VS. DEMOCRATIC REPUBLICANS

Gradually, these issues and views became the core of two distinct parties. Around Hamilton gathered leaders and followers who soon took the name Federalists. Eventually Washington became closely identified with the Federalist party. On the other side were the Anti-Federalists or Democratic-Republicans (not to be confused with the modern day parties bearing these names). Their chief spokesmen were Jefferson, Madison, and John Taylor, all Virginians.

FRANCOPHILES VS. ANGLOPHILES

The two emerging parties also came to take different stands on foreign policy.

Anglo-American relations remained sour long after the 1783 Treaty of Paris. If the British weren't exactly sore losers, they weren't shy about exhibiting their pique. Britain, as we saw, refused to allow Americans to trade freely with the crown's West Indies colonies and continued to occupy military posts in the Western part of American territory, pending the repayment of debts. Meanwhile in New Orleans, Spain denied the right of deposit to American western farmers, while France, despite its alliance and commercial treaty with the United States, also seemed unwilling to concede trading rights to American shippers.

THE FRENCH REVOLUTION

Matters became infinitely worse and more complex after the outbreak of the French Revolution in mid-1789. Most Americans welcomed the upheaval in France initially. But slowly the revolution abroad came under the control of zealots and extremists who instituted a reign of terror against the Revolution's enemies, executed the king and queen, and attacked the Christian religion. In 1792, France declared war on Austria and Prussia and early the next year on Great Britain, Spain, and Holland. How would the United States respond to the events in Europe, especially in light of the Franco-American alliance of 1778? Despite the excesses of the French revolutionary leaders, Jefferson and his party continued to favor France. Hamilton and his associates, however, came to see France as the source of atheism and a dangerous disrespect for social order. They perceived Britain as a citadel of civilization. President Washington responded to the outbreak of war by declaring the United States neutral and urging Americans to avoid hostile acts against either side.

But the French, fishing for allies, were not willing to accept American neutrality. In April 1793 the French Republic made citizen Edmond Genêt its minister to the United States with the assignment of obtaining the Americans' diplomatic and military support. Genêt, giving rich new meaning to the word "chutzpah," was soon commissioning American privateers to attack British ships and organizing a military expedition from American soil against British and Spanish possessions in North America.

Even for Jefferson, this was a bit much, and he agreed that Genêt had to go. Soon after, Jefferson came to feel that he had lost the president's ear in foreign policy to his cabinet rival, the illegitimate New Yorker, Alexander

CITIZEN GENÊT

Edmond Genêt was, arguably, the most undiplomatic diplomat in the history of diplomacy. He'd already been declared *persona non grata* and thrown out of St. Petersburg by the Russians, so when he started debating and insulting everyone in the American government, including President Washington, they shouldn't have been surprised. When Jefferson finally decided to get rid of him, Genêt's successor arrived with orders to arrest him and bring him back to France for trial. In an ironic twist, the U.S. refused to extradite him. The unstoppable Genêt then became a naturalized American citizen, eventually marrying Cornelia Clinton, the daughter of the governor of New York, and, after her death, Martha Osgood, the daughter of the first postmaster general. A survivor, wouldn't you say?

Hamilton, and resigned as Secretary of State. Before long new problems with Britain surfaced. In the West, Americans charged, the British were inciting the Indians to rebel, and "impressing" into their own navy any U.S. seamen captured afloat. To Americans, such impressment was a violation of sovereignty and a national humiliation. Over the next twenty years neutral rights in times of armed conflict would become a major issue as France, Britain, and their respective allies fought an epic war that encompassed the globe.

FOREIGN TREATIES

In June 1794, Washington sent Chief Justice John Jay to England to resolve Anglo-American differences. He might as well not have bothered. The British agreed to evacuate the garrisons in the northwestern part of North America and made some minor trade concessions to the

United States. The two countries also agreed to a joint commission to settle unpaid debts owed British creditors. But nothing was put in writing to resolve the issues of impressment, the Indian problem, or Loyalist claims.

What little Jay did accomplish got him nothing but abuse back home. Virginians, who owed much of the unpaid British debt, saw Jay's treaty as a blow to their interests. Merchants considered it too feeble to solve their trade problems. The Anti-Federalists called it a sellout to Britain. Wherever Jay traveled after his return he was greeted by effigies of himself dangling from nooses. So long as the dummies weren't actually on fire, he could hope that he could take the mass hatred in stride. Despite the public outcry, Hamilton and the more ardent Federalists defended the agreement and its provisions were adopted.

Most successful were the negotiations with Spain over navigation of the Mississippi and other differences. By the 1795 Treaty of San Lorenzo (Pinckney's Treaty), Spain agreed to allow the United States the right of deposit at New Orleans for three years subject to renewal, and agreed that the Mississippi would be the western boundary of the U.S. and the 31st parallel (with Florida below it) would be the Southern boundary, as specified in the 1783 Treaty of Paris.

THE ADAMS ADMINISTRATION

Washington had been unanimously reelected to a second term in 1792. (A more recent George in the White House was not so lucky.) He could have remained in office for life but he decided that two terms were enough and refused to run again in 1796. In September 1796 he composed a "Farewell Address" (one never actually spoken aloud, and in fact probably written, and certainly

"Al, would I lie to you on Washington's Birthday?"

radically edited, by Alexander Hamilton) saying goodbye to his fellow citizens. In this document he laid out his reasons for declining a third term, deplored political partisanship, urged honest repayment of the debt, and advised the nation to steer clear of permanent—though not temporary—alliances with foreign countries.

Later that year the presidential electors chose vice-president John Adams to succeed Washington and gave Jefferson the vice-presidency. These men were the leaders of the two opposing parties, but the Constitution as then written merely provided that the person with the most electoral votes would be president; the one with the second largest number vice-president.

THE XYZ AFFAIR, OR
THE FRENCH KISS-OFF

Adams's single term would be dominated by foreign policy issues. Angry at the supposedly pro-British Jay

Treaty, the French went into a snit, refusing to receive the new American ambassador when he arrived in December 1796. To improve relations, Adams sent three American commissioners to Paris. When they arrived they were held at arm's length by Talleyrand, the French foreign minister, whose agents, designated in American dispatches as X, Y, and Z, demanded a U.S. loan to France and a $240,000 bribe before talking. The Americans were put off by this behavior and refused. The negotiations broke off. In April 1798 Adams released the XYZ correspondence to disclose French perfidy. (One of the American commissioners, Charles Cotesworth Pinckney, had indignantly rejected the bribe suggestion with: "No, no, not a sixpence." This was not too colorful and the press, despite Pinckney's denials changed it to: "Millions for defense but not a cent for tribute." Pinckney always denied the words but they were put on his gravestone despite him.) A wave of indignation swept the country and even Republicans denounced Talleyrand and the French government.

For two years, U.S. and French sabers rattled in their scabbards. Congress established a Navy Department and unilaterally repealed the revolutionary war treaties with France. The administration recalled Washington to serve as commanding general of the armed forces with Hamilton as his second in command. The U.S. and France were soon involved in a series of naval engagements in the Caribbean that amounted to de facto war. Fortunately, worse conflict was avoided so that today the only French stockades in the Caribbean belong to Club Med. Adams sent an American emissary to France, and the resulting Convention of 1800 formally released the United States from its obligations under the revolutionary war treaties. Thereafter Franco-American relations improved, to the point where today you can actually be served a turkey "croissant" at 30,000 feet as you fly from Chicago to Phoenix.

THE ALIEN AND SEDITION ACTS

While international relations improved, at home the party battles became more heated. It was difficult for the Federalists to accept the legitimacy of their critics' attacks. Adams and his colleagues considered the pro-French Republicans to be agents of dangerous atheistic, radical ideas. Many of the most vocal pro-French critics of the U.S. administration were foreign refugees, a fact that made their attacks all the more obnoxious. In 1798 the Federalist Congress passed a series of measures, the Alien and Sedition Acts, to quiet these dissident voices. Without even waiting for final passage of the Alien Act a flock of panicky foreigners fled the United States. Under the Sedition Act, at least 25 Americans were prosecuted for seeking to undermine the government. Ten, all Republican editors or printers, were convicted.

In 1798–99 the Republican-controlled legislatures of Kentucky and Virginia passed resolutions denouncing

THE AMERICAN CIVIL LIBERTIES UNION'S WORST NIGHTMARE

The first three of the Alien and Sedition laws lengthened the period for naturalization, allowed the president to expel all aliens suspected of "treasonable" inclinations, and gave him authority to arrest or banish enemy aliens in time of war. The fourth, the Sedition Act, was a formula for tyranny. It made it a crime for either citizens or aliens to join together to oppose execution of federal laws, to try to prevent a federal officer from performing his duties, or to aid, or attempt to commit, insurrection, riot, or "unlawful assembly." Any person who sought to slander or bring into disrepute the American government, Congress, or the President, could be heavily fined or imprisoned.

the Alien and Sedition Acts as measures that exceeded the rights accorded to Congress by the Constitution. One of the Kentucky resolutions further declared that the "rightful remedy" against such usurpations was "nullification" of the law in question by the individual states. Both states proclaimed their loyalty to the Union but the Resolutions would provide precedents for the states' rights views by which the South would eventually justify secession from the union.

The voters repudiated John Adams and the Federalists in the 1800 presidential election. Adams's opponents were Republicans Jefferson and Aaron Burr of New York. Under Article II of the Constitution the candidate with the highest number of votes became president; the next highest, vice-president. The Republicans clearly intended the "Sage of Monticello" to be their presidential candidate and Burr their vice-presidential choice. But there was a goof-up and both Republicans got 73 votes to Adams's 65 (and 64 for the Federalist vice-presidential candidate Charles C. Pinckney). The Republicans as a party had clearly won, but who would now actually be president and who vice-president?

Under the rules, the Federalist-controlled House of Representatives would have to decide. For reasons made clear below, if Burr had had his way, the solution might have been pistols at dawn. In the House, a majority of Federalist congressmen at first resolved to go for Burr, but Hamilton, now a private citizen but still a power in the party, opposed him. Jefferson, he said, at least had "some pretensions to character," whereas Burr was "bankrupt beyond redemption." (This was the sort of remark that could get you dead at the time: Burr shot and killed Hamilton in a duel in July 1804.) Hamilton's views in the end prevailed. On the 36th ballot Jefferson was chosen president.

And so Jefferson, leader of the Republicans, would be-

Hamilton and Burr face off. Burr's aim was better.

FIGHTING WORDS

What to an early nineteenth-century politician were fighting words, today would be considered nothing worse than the contents of a mildly negative political ad on TV. Burr and Hamilton had a long history of saying unpleasant things about each other, and neither trusted the other as far as he could throw him, but the words that actually resulted in their famous duel were pretty mild. Seems Hamilton said Burr was "dangerous" and allowed further that he "could detail . . . a still more despicable opinion." Burr asked for an explanation of these words, Hamilton didn't have one ready, and the duel was on: ten paces in, of all places, Weehawken, New Jersey (since dueling was illegal in New York). The duel killed Hamilton, and destroyed Burr's social and political reputation.

come the third president of the United States. It might not seem like a big deal today, but this was a landmark: the first time in the history of modern government that power had been transferred democratically from a party in power to one that wasn't. Now, what would the new administration do with its mandate to rule?

SUMMARY

The Articles of Confederation provided a weak central government that was unable to pay its debts because it had no power to tax. The individual states, lacking a central authority, were little more than a collection of commercially warring mini-nations.

The Constitutional Convention of 1787 was called to establish an effective central government. The men who attended the Convention were an elite group that aimed to create a government of the elite.

The Bill of Rights was intended to limit the powers of the Federal government over states and over citizens. It answered the concerns of states who hesitated to ratify a document (the Constitution) that so strengthened the federal government.

Opposition in the states to the Alien and Sedition Acts, passed by a Federalist Congress, became the basis for later assertions of states' rights, and eventually secession.

The nation demonstrated its maturity when Jefferson succeeded Adams as president and, for the first time in modern history, power was transferred democratically from one political party to another.

CHAPTER 4

EXPANSION AND WAR:
THE NEW NATION'S BAPTISM OF FIRE

YOU MUST REMEMBER THIS

The War of 1812 demonstrated to Americans that they could beat the best armies of Europe—and vividly showed the error of the old Republican idea that having a passive federal government was the best policy.

IMPORTANT EVENTS

- ★ Marbury V. Madison, 1803
- ★ The Louisiana Purchase, 1803
- ★ The Chesapeake incident and the Embargo Act, 1807
- ★ Madison elected president, 1808
- ★ The British burn the Capitol, 1814
- ★ Battle of New Orleans, 1815
- ★ Treaty of Ghent, 1815

THE ATTACK ON FEDERALISM

Thomas Jefferson's inaugural address in 1801 encouraged a spirit of national unity. "We are all Republicans, we are all Federalists," he declared, speaking with a magnanimity that is easier to feign when you've just won. But party rivalry and party war intruded almost from the outset of his administration.

Just before the new administration took over, the Federalist Congress created a flock of new federal judiciary offices. The Republicans were wise to this move. These "midnight appointments" were an attempt to entrench Federalist principles in the one branch of government their opponents could still control, and they resolved to undo them.

Thomas Jefferson (1743–1826). Farmer, scientist, statesman, author. This depicts one of the few occasions when he had time to twiddle his thumbs.

Jefferson refused to deliver the official commissions to several of the midnight appointees. Four of them, including William Marbury, sued in the federal courts to compel the government to comply. In 1803 the decision in *Marbury v. Madison,* rendered by Chief Justice John Marshall, established one of the most important principles of Constitutional law: that the Supreme Court has the right to decide which laws passed by Congress are constitutional and which are not. Marshall was a true-blue Federalist, but he avoided a head-on clash with the administration. The Court had no jurisdiction in the Marbury suit, he said. In effect, the administration had won. But only on the narrow point of Marbury's suit. An earlier congressional judiciary measure, Marshall declared, was unconstitutional and

BEHIND THE SCENES

Little-Known Players and Unsung Heroes

People, few of them white males, who don't always make it into the history books.

Tenskwatawa (1768–c.1834).
"The Prophet," a brother of Tecumseh, a Shawnee religious leader with a wide following, precipitated the disastrous battle at Tippecanoe in his brother's absence.

Sequoyah (c.1770–1843).
A Cherokee who developed a written alphabet for the Cherokee language, allowing Cherokee speakers to read and write.

Sacagawea (c. 1786–1812).
A Hidatsa Indian woman who served as an interpreter for Lewis and Clark to the Shoshone and other tribes. Probably, along with Pocahontas, the best known of all Indian women.

Black Hawk (1767–1838).
In 1831, he invaded his old homeland in Illinois, resulting in the Black Hawk War, a relatively minor military incident made more famous by the fact that Abraham Lincoln served in it as a captain of volunteers.

Paul Cuffe (1759–1817).
A self-made merchant sailor, and the first American black to achieve substantial wealth. In 1815, convinced that separation was the only solution to the race problem in America, he transported a group of American blacks to Sierra Leone.

BEHIND THE SCENES

(*continued*)

Denmark Vesey (1767–1822).
A slave who bought his freedom after winning a lottery. He organized an elaborate, though abortive, uprising among South Carolina slaves. His plot was exposed before it was executed, and he was hanged, despite the fact that the rebellion had never happened.

Chief Justice John Marshall (1755–1835).

hence null and void. This was "judicial review," a principle that Federalists supported and Republicans deplored.

Though forced to concede the judiciary to their opponents, the Jeffersonians kept right on taking potshots at the Federalist program. They repealed what remained of the Alien and Sedition Acts still in force, sold off the

DON'T TRY TOO HARD TO GET WHAT YOU WANT . . . BECAUSE YOU JUST MIGHT GET IT

Even though the Republicans "won" in *Marbury v. Madison,* the decision established the principle of "judicial review," an idea supported by Federalists and not by Republicans. This was the first time that the Supreme Court had ever nullified an act of Congress, a move so daring that the Court would not repeat it for more than fifty years. But what most people view today as the essential mission of the Supreme Court—to decide the constitutionality of laws passed by Congress—had been firmly established.

**WHO'S
H
O**

> ## Do These Names Ring a Bell?
>
> 🌂 **John Marshall** (1755–1835).
> Chief justice of the Supreme Court, 1801–1835. Most famous for establishing doctrine of judicial review in *Marbury v. Madison*.
>
> 🌂 **James Madison** (1751–1836).
> Fourth president of the United States, leader of Jeffersonian Republican party. Secretary of State under Jefferson, elected president in 1809.

government's stock in the Bank of the United States, replaced Federalist officials with Republicans, and contracted the federal debt by slashing the budget.

THE JEFFERSONIANS AND FOREIGN AFFAIRS

In foreign relations, however, Jefferson ignored the Republican principle of minimal government. He dispatched an American naval force to discipline Tripoli, one of the Barbary States (Tripoli, Algiers, Tunis, and Morocco) which had long preyed on American commerce and taken American hostages. This gave the marines a line for their hymn, but it was not until 1816 that the other Barbary States desisted from their piratical actions against American commerce. Clearly, piracy and hostage-taking are among the Middle East's more venerable traditions.

Jefferson was also a territorial expansionist who saw the vast, "empty" West as a future home for American farmers. So long as land was available, the United States would remain wedded to agriculture and avoid the dangerous social and economic changes that Hamilton sought to encourage. He soon had his chance to put his money where his mouth was.

In 1800 the Louisiana Territory, including New Orleans, had been secretly ceded by Spain to France, which under its new ruler, Napoleon Bonaparte, planned to reestablish a French empire in America. The transfer, to say the least, profoundly disturbed the American government. It was one thing to have the area under the control of powerless Spain, but quite another to have Napoleon free to work his will in the American West. Louisiana might forever block American westward development, and French control of New Orleans threatened the exit point of river-borne commerce on the Mississippi and its tributaries. If France held New Orleans, said

"So tell me. How were you 'ere you saw Elba?"

YEAH, BUT HE DIDN'T HAVE NANCY REAGAN AS FIRST LADY, EITHER.
·····························
Jefferson preferred Republican "simplicity" to the "monarchical" pomp and circumstance that surrounded the Federalist president. Rather than delivering his annual message to Congress in person, for example, Jefferson sent both houses his written text. He also avoided stiff, formal state dinners. Instead, the president dined with friends at a round table where no guest took precedence. Often he served the food himself, and, said his enemies, he did not always wear a clean shirt (eighteenth-century grunge?).

Jefferson (no lover of Britain), ". . . we must marry ourselves to the British fleet and nation."

In early 1803 Jefferson opened negotiations to buy New Orleans and West Florida, the panhandle along the Gulf Coast. He lucked out. Napoleon had already decided to get rid of his holdings in America because they were too vulnerable to British attack if war resumed in Europe. He decided to unload the whole thing while he could still get some money for it. So he offered the Americans not only New Orleans, but the entire Louisiana Territory for $15 million. You didn't have to be Donald Trump to recognize the best real estate deal since the Dutch bought Manhattan, and the pleasantly surprised Americans jumped on it. So what if no one was quite sure of Louisiana's boundaries? It practically doubled the size of the country!

THE ROAD TO WAR

While Napoleon and the British duked it out in Europe, America asserted neutrality. At the same time, American merchants were making plenty of money supplying the French. Grumman Aircraft they weren't, but it just goes to show war profiteering is the world's second oldest profession. Under the stimulus of war, the American merchant marine had ballooned, with hundreds of ships and thousands of mariners, many lured from British service, plying European and Caribbean waters. Britain, naturally, didn't care for this, and began stopping American ships on the high seas, both to remove British deserters and to seize material headed for France. Whatever the merits of the British position—and let's face it, they did have a case—Americans were outraged. In early 1806 the U.S. Senate passed a resolution calling British seizures "an unprovoked aggression" and a "violation of neutral rights." Congress enacted the first Non-Importation Act excluding a long list of British goods from the American market.

In June, 1807, the British frigate *H.M.S. Leopard* overhauled an American naval vessel, the *U.S.S. Chesapeake,* to search for deserters from the Royal Navy. This was the first time the British had ever stopped an American naval vessel, and the shooting started. A number of Americans were killed, and self-righteous or not, anti-British feelings swept the towns and cities. War seemed imminent. In 1807, with Jefferson's support, Congress passed the Embargo Act, ending all U.S. commerce with foreign nations. While the South and West could accept this and be patriotic (what the hell, it didn't cost them anything), the merchants, shipbuilders, sail makers, and mariners of the Northeast protested. Smuggling was followed by anti-smuggling laws, which were followed by—you guessed it—more ingenious smuggling. Just before leaving office, Jefferson gave up and signed the repeal of the Embargo Act, reopening trade with all nations except Britain and France.

MADISON AS PRESIDENT

The "Father of the Constitution," James Madison, proved a naive and ineffective chief executive. Washington Irving called him "a withered little applejohn," and, however cruel the characterization, Madison was in fact a wizened little man lacking in vigor and innocent in the extreme.

In 1810, he fell into a diplomatic trap laid by the wily Napoleon. Groping for a formula that would punish our enemies without hurting ourselves, Congress had passed Macon's Bill Number 2. The effect of this bill was to get the United States to reimpose an embargo on Britain while removing one on France. Britain responded as you might expect them to, and before long American and British ships were lobbing cannon shots at one another on the high seas.

Meanwhile, in the Northwest, the Shawnee chief Tecumseh was leading an uprising against land grabs by settlers in Ohio, Indiana, and Michigan. In 1811 William Henry Harrison, governor of Indiana Territory, sent a force against Tecumseh, winning an ambiguous victory at Tippecanoe—with Tecumseh escaping to fight another day. Rather than attribute their problems to their own greed, the settlers decided to blame the British for

TIPPECANOE

You might have guessed that the word has nothing to do with canoes that tip over, but you probably don't know what it does mean. Tippecanoe was the name of a river in Indiana that flows into the Wabash, and is the name of the county where the battle of Tippecanoe took place, but in fact, no one's quite sure what the origin of the name is. Best guess is that it comes from a Potowatomie word that means "buffalo fish," but don't ask us what a buffalo fish is.

inciting the Indians, and resolved to expel the Limeys from North America. They sent a bunch of "War Hawks" to Congress led by the Speaker of the House Henry Clay of Kentucky. Clay demanded a larger army and navy, and threatened to oppose Madison's re-election if he did not push for war. On June 1, 1812, Madison gave in to them, sending a war message to Congress citing American trading rights, impressment, and the incitement of the Indians on the frontier as reasons for action. Eighteen days later Congress declared war.

THE WAR OF 1812

"Would you like to come up to my place and see my War of 1812 medals?"

Britain was 3,000 miles away in a major war with France, and the U.S. had more manpower than British Canada, yet the American army was small, poorly equipped, and badly led, and the British navy was far more powerful than the American. The Americans were not in great financial shape, either, and public opinion was split, with New England strongly opposed to fighting "Mr. Madison's War."

Canada was the obvious point at which to attack the enemy—that was where the British were, after all—and Canada would make a splendid addition to America's already princely domain. But American commanders and troops were not up to the job. In the summer of 1812, for example, General William Hull surrendered Detroit to invading Canadians without firing a shot. An American attack aimed at Montreal stalled when the New York militia claimed that they were not required to serve outside their home state, and refused to cross the Canadian border.

Military successes by American frigates at sea sustained American morale during a dark period, but they did not prevent the British navy from effectively blockading American ports and running most of America's commerce off the seas.

Matters improved in 1813. Oliver Perry defeated a British flotilla on Lake Erie, ("We have met the enemy and they are ours" said his famous dispatch) and William Henry Harrison subdued the British and their ally Tecumseh in the Battle of the Thames. The Northwest was now safe from British attack.

TECUMSEH

Chief Tecumseh (1768–1813).

A Shawnee chief renowned for his eloquence and organizational abilities, Tecumseh spent his entire life a warrior. When he began to organize all the Indians from Canada to Florida in a league, Governor of Indiana William Henry Harrison was alarmed—particularly so since Tecumseh asserted his right to approve any further deals that turned over Indian land to the U.S. Harrison, of course, objected, so he decided on a preemptive strike. Tecumseh's organization never recovered from their defeat at Tippecanoe. The British knew a good ally when they saw one, though, and in the War of 1812 Tecumseh held a commission as a brigadier-general in the British army. Harrison later caught up with him again at the Battle of the Thames, and this time Tecumseh was killed.

The Gilbert Stuart portrait of George Washington that Dolly Madison saved from being burned by the British.

In mid-August 1814 a force of 4,000 veteran British troops freed from fighting in France landed at the mouth of the Patuxent River in Maryland and marched on Washington. The British burned the Capitol, the White House, and other government buildings right down to the ground, but all was not lost: Dolly Madison saved the Gilbert Stuart portrait of George Washington.

The firebugs proceeded to Baltimore where the bombardment of Fort McHenry failed to secure them the town. However, it did inspire Francis Scott Key to write the national anthem. Indeed, the actual flag that proudly did wave can still be seen: in an exhibit hall in Washington, D.C.'s Smithsonian Institution. The British then climbed aboard their transports and departed for the West Indies.

Just before Christmas of 1814 American and British commissioners meeting in the Belgian town of Ghent signed a peace treaty—too late, though, to stop a major battle at New Orleans, which Wellington had targeted.

The British, as the popular song goes, ran so fast that the hounds couldn't catch 'em down the Mississippi to the Gulf of Mexico. But with a force of Kentucky and Tennessee riflemen, free blacks, and followers of the pirate Jean Lafitte, Andrew Jackson stopped the British attack dead. Hidden behind breastworks made of cotton bales, the Americans laid down a deadly barrage of rifle and artillery fire against the advancing British regulars. Two thousand redcoats, including their commander Sir Edward Packenham, died in the battle, with American casualties limited to eight killed and thirteen wounded. New Orleans was the greatest American victory of the war. It made a hero of Jackson, a Tennessee planter-politician of humble birth, and catapulted him into national prominence. It also transformed the public mood from gloom to joy.

Nationalism soared. The United States, it was clear, could beat the best that Europe could send against it. The war had also shown that many of the policies of the old Republicans regarding federal powers had been mistaken. Poor roads had handicapped the American military effort. So had the absence of a central bank. Many Americans would now see virtue in policies they and their party had long deplored.

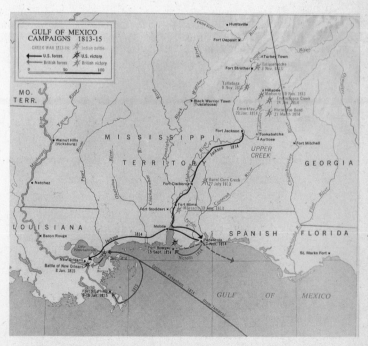

This map depicts pivotal campaigns in the Gulf of Mexico region during the War of 1812.

The peace treaty itself, news of which reached the U.S. on February 11, 1815, ignored questions of neutral rights, of the western Indians, of boundary problems. It settled nothing that the United States had fought for. Still, peace was better than war and Americans could now resume their normal lives with a heightened sense of their national destiny.

SUMMARY

In 1803, for the first time, the Supreme Court nullified an act of Congress, setting the precedent for judicial review.

Jefferson's purchase of Louisiana from France marked the beginning of American expansion toward the West—the vast "unpopulated" region that Jefferson saw as the future home of American farmers.

American victory in the War of 1812, though inconclusive politically, gave rise to a new American nationalism.

CHAPTER 5

SEA TO SHINING SEA:
THE ERA OF GOOD FEELINGS

YOU MUST REMEMBER THIS

By 1840, the political division between Whigs and Democrats had been firmly established. Whigs favored an activist federal government, Democrats favored states' rights. Whigs wanted government to intervene forcefully in the economy, Democrats favored laissez-faire. To some extent the differences reflected a division between North and South that would ultimately tear the nation apart.

IMPORTANT EVENTS

- ★ James Monroe elected president, 1816
- ★ The Missouri Compromise, 1819
- ★ The Adams-Onis Treaty, 1819
- ★ The Monroe Doctrine, 1823
- ★ John Quincy Adams elected president, 1824
- ★ Erie Canal opens, 1825
- ★ Andrew Jackson elected president, 1828

THE ERA OF GOOD FEELINGS

The patriotic surge after the Battle of New Orleans devastated the Federalists. They had originally been the more nationalist of the two parties, but the anti-war stand of Federalist New England and the anti-government carping of Federalist critics elsewhere had branded the party as treasonous. Its support soon melted away.

Meanwhile, the Republicans had stolen their opponents political clothes. In his December 1815 message to Congress, President Madison called for a federal program to build roads and canals, a protective tariff, and "a national seminary of learning" in Washington to create strong "national sentiments" among young Americans. In 1816 the Republican Congress passed a major tariff act to protect American industry against the cheaper labor and greater efficiency of British industry and chartered a Second Bank of the United States with a larger capital than the first. Congress also approved Calhoun's Bonus Bill to use the proceeds of Bank of the U.S. (BUS) profits for "internal improvements," a term that described the building of roads, canals, and other projects to improve transportation.

James Monroe (1758–1831).

The presidential election of 1816 saw the overwhelming victory of another Virginian, James Monroe, over the Federalist candidate Rufus King of New York. King carried only Massachusetts, Connecticut, and Delaware in the electoral college. And Federalist decline would continue. In 1820, Monroe ran without opposition of any sort.

The Federalists, except for a few small pockets of diehards, were now defunct and the nation's "first party

WHO'S
H
O ☛

Do These Names Ring a Bell?

☙ **James Monroe** (1758-1831).
Fifth president of the United States. Governor of Virginia 1799-1802, secretary of state 1811-1817, secretary of war 1814-1815. Elected president in 1816 and re-elected in 1820.

☙ **John Quincy Adams** (1767-1848).
What's in a name? Well, let's just say that, for the Adamses, the presidency became the family business. President like his father before him (sixth president, to be exact), secretary of state under Monroe, Adams fils served one term as president, and then became an anti-slavery congressman, 1839-1848.

☙ **Andrew Jackson** (1767-1845).
Seventh president of the United States (Old Hickory to his friends). A major-general in the army, he made his reputation fighting Indians in Alabama and Florida. First governor of Florida, then a senator, and elected president in 1828 and again in 1832.

☙ **Henry Clay** (1777-1852).
A "War Hawk" in Congress before the War of 1812, he participated in negotiating the Treaty of Ghent which ended the war. Secretary of state in 1825, senator 1831-1842, unsuccessful candidate for president in 1832 and 1844.

☙ **Nicholas Biddle** (1786-1844).
Director of the Bank of the United States.

system" had run its course. This does not mean that politics had disappeared, however. Political contention continued in the states and in Washington in the form of jockeying for advantage and intra-cabinet intrigues. But it did not take the form of party politics. And this trend away from organized politics was reflected in election turnouts. Each year fewer voters came to the polls to rubber stamp the candidates chosen by party caucuses or state legislatures.

BEHIND THE SCENES

Little-Known Players and Unsung Heroes

People, few of them white males, who don't always make it into the history books.

Nat Turner (1800-1831).
A deeply religious Virginia slave, he rebelled with a group of followers, killing more than fifty whites before being captured and executed.

Elias Howe (1819-1867).
Inventor of the sewing machine.

Gail Borden (1801-1874).
Developer of a method for processing food that allowed the production of such products as condensed milk. No matter what the textbooks say, his interest in Elsie the Cow was purely platonic.

Samuel F. B. Morse (1791-1872).
The inventor of the telegraph.

John Deere (1804-1886).
The inventor of the steel plow. His company's

BEHIND THE SCENES

(*continued*)

eventual development of the sit-down lawn-mower denied yet another form of exercise to sedentary suburban males.

Robert Owen (1771-1858).
English industrialist and philanthropist who founded a socialist utopian community at New Harmony, Indiana in 1824, which led to the establishment of many similar communities, none of which had much luck in overcoming the innate materialistic tendencies of the American spirit.

Frances Wright (1795-1852).
Writer, founder of a utopian community, proponent of birth control, sexual freedom, and the emancipation of women. Whether the recidivist chauvinist males of the nineteenth century were aroused or just plain scared by her activities is not entirely clear.

THE NEW WEST

During this "Era of Good Feelings" much of the nation's attention was directed to "settling" the West—that is, taking land from the Indians and moving in. The government policy of transferring the trans-Appalachian Indian tribes to the region beyond the Mississippi was ruthless.

In the Southeast, the sense of urgency was compounded by the development of a cotton culture based

IT'S GOT NOTHING TO DO WITH TONIC

You probably first heard the term "cotton gin" in fourth grade. But what's a "gin"? We thought you'd never ask. The answer is simple: "gin" is short for "engine."

Eli Whitney's cotton gin.

on short staple cotton that could be grown inland and harvested on the "gin" invented by Eli Whitney in 1793 that removed its sticky seeds.

The cotton belt soon spread all across the Gulf Plain and southern half of the Mississippi Valley, making it one of the richest parts of the nation. The rise of the "Cotton Kingdom" soon gave the faltering "peculiar institution" of chattel slavery a new lease on life.

Of course, the Indians didn't think much of this expansionism, and put up a fight. In the North the Sauk and Fox Indians were subdued in the Black Hawk War (1831-32) which cleared Illinois and Wisconsin for white farmers. In the South the Cherokee, Choctaw, Creek, and Chickasaw were expelled from their lands by a combination of chicanery and coercion. Driven west to Indian Territory by soldiers, during the winter of 1838, many hundreds of Cherokee perished on the Trail of Tears. In Florida the Seminoles resisted and were only subdued after years of war and the expenditure of millions of dollars.

Indian resistance did not hold up settlement of the Northwest and Southwest for long. Thousands of settlers moved across the mountains to start farms and take up residence in flourishing new cities. Between 1812 and 1837, nine new states were admitted to the Union.

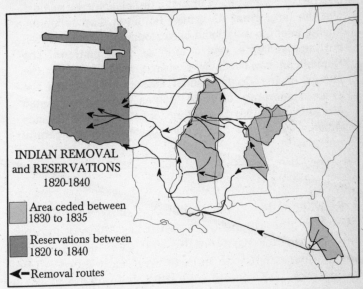

INDIAN REMOVAL
and RESERVATIONS
1820-1840

Area ceded between
1830 to 1835

Reservations between
1820 to 1840

←─ Removal routes

This map depicts the routes and areas used by the U.S. government to remove Native Americans from the lands they'd lived on long before the U.S. government was even a gleam in Thomas Jefferson's great-great-grandfather's eye.

THE MISSOURI COMPROMISE

In 1819 Missouri, a part of the Louisiana Purchase territory, applied for statehood as a slave state. At the same time, the residents of Maine, previously a part of Massachusetts, became restless for separate statehood. In 1819, Congress took up consideration of admitting both to the Union.

GOOD FEELINGS
. . . .

The period from 1816 to 1824 is often called the "Era of Good Feelings"—and it was the Republicans who felt best, since the Federalist party had virtually disappeared. Of course many of these Republicans were more like the late, great Alexander Hamilton than Jefferson, having adopted a national bank, federally financed internal improvements, and a tariff as their platform. The Republican candidate was always a shoo-in, and the choice of the Congressional leaders was always the present secretary of state—James Monroe succeeded Madison, and his secretary of state, John Quincy Adams, succeeded him. Cozy, but not rousing electoral politics.

Representative James Tallmadge of New York introduced an amendment to the Missouri statehood bill prohibiting further slaves in the state-to-be and providing for gradual emancipation of those already there. All hell broke loose. The South had fallen behind the North in population, and thus in representation in the House. But with the same number of slave and free states, the South still had equal representation in the Senate. If Tallmadge's amendment passed, the South would be consigned to permanent minority status in the federal legislature. Congress, said the South, had no right to make "free-soil" a condition of entering the Union. Northerners said that Congress not only had the right, but the duty to exclude slavery in every new state.

The result of the dispute was the Missouri Compromise: Maine would enter the Union as a free state, Missouri as a slave state thus preserving for the time equal numbers of free and slave states. The remainder of the Louisiana Purchase Territory would be divided along the

36-30' line of latitude with slavery forbidden north of it, but allowed south of it.

Though sectional peace was preserved, the angry debate seemed ominous. The aging Thomas Jefferson called the Missouri debate "a fire bell in the night," warning of serious danger to the Union ahead.

IRON HORSES AND A MULE NAMED SAL

Getting around in nineteenth-century America wasn't easy. In the East, you could always go by boat—Benjamin Franklin, for example, moved to Philadelphia from Boston and took a schooner to get there. Once you got away from the coast, though, you had big problems. There were no traffic jams, of course, but that's only because there were no roads. The Mississippi and its tributaries weren't bad—provided you were going with the current. Flat boats and rafts moving with the current could carry goods to American coastal cities and to Europe fairly cheaply. But if you wanted to ship goods the other way—say, from New York to Cincinnati—things weren't so convenient. You had to go by ocean vessel to New Orleans, and then get a keel boat to pole up the river against the current. That, obviously, was slow, hard, and expensive, and, arguably, more effort than a trip to Cincinnati was worth.

Turnpikes, then as now, were the first response. In 1808 the Federal government began a major road project beginning at Cumberland, Maryland, and reaching Vandalia, Illinois, 700 miles away some 42 years later. This span of time was long enough, in theory (if not in reality) for a long-lived civil engineer who helped start the project to see a son and grandson each become old enough to work with him on the roadway. And you thought it took your local highway department a long time to fix potholes!

Next came canals, inspired by the successful completion by New York State in 1825 of the Erie Canal connecting the Hudson at Albany with Lake Erie. This route not only immortalized in song a mule named Sal, but reduced shipping costs greatly in both directions, and made New York City the booming center of increased trade in manufactured goods from Europe and in grain, pork, and beef from the West.

New York's good fortune set off a canal craze in other Atlantic cities and in western farming regions as well, though few of them made much money. And steamboats—paddle-wheelers like Fulton's legendary Clermont—also helped move goods cheaply, even against the current. Now you could get from New York City to Albany in just 62 hours, a distance that requires about three hours today, unless it's rush hour, in which case the earlier figure may apply. Before long, steamboats

The Erie Canal at Lockport, New York.
Can you find Sal the mule?

THE INDUSTRIAL REVOLUTION AND
OFFICE AUTOMATION;
The Water Powered Stapler

were plying the waters of the Mississippi and all its more navigable branches.

But water transport had its drawbacks. In the North the streams and canals often froze in the winter. In the summer low water and snags hampered river navigation. The solution was the "iron horse." In the early 1830s the first trains pulled by steam locomotives began to run out of Charleston, Baltimore, and Boston. By 1840 there were over 3,300 miles of track in the United States. The most exuberant period of railroad construction still lay ahead, yet by the 1840s the nation was well on its way to possessing an integrated system of cheap transportation to tie the states together.

THE INDUSTRIAL REVOLUTION

The most momentous economic change of these years was the advent of the machinery-run factory. It was in

England that steam engines, power looms, and automatic spinning machines, all joined under one roof, first began to spew out cheap textiles for consumers. Britain was not unaware of the strategic value of this technology, and

---

SPEAKING ONLY TO LOWELLS: A QUICK GLANCE AT THE L'S IN HARVARD'S ALUMNI DIRECTORY

John Lowell, 1743-1802.
Jurist, member of the Massachusetts Constitutional Convention.

John Lowell, 1769-1840.
Son of the first John Lowell, jurist, pamphleteer.

James Russell Lowell, 1819-1891.
Diplomat, author, journalist, first editor of The *Atlantic Monthly*.

Percival Lowell, 1855-1916.
Amy's and Abbott's brother. Writer and astronomer, founder of the Lowell Observatory in Flagstaff, Arizona.

Abbott Lawrence Lowell, 1856-1943.
Educator, lawyer, author, president of Harvard University.

Amy Lowell, 1874-1925.
Poet, literary critic, and biographer of Keats. Sister of Abbott and Percival, and the only one of the bunch who didn't go to Harvard, for obvious reasons.

Robert Lowell (1917-1977).
Mid-twentieth century "confessional" poet (his mommy drove him to it). Lured away from Harvard by John Crowe Ransom and the *Kenyon Review*.

THE LOWELL GIRLS

Francis Cabot Lowell's factories employed mostly young women "operatives" drawn from rural New England. The "Lowell girls" were chaperoned closely and housed in attractive dormitories. They were paid relatively well and enjoyed the use of company-supplied churches, libraries, and lecture halls. They published their own newspaper and literary magazine. In short they were, forgive the expression, a close-knit bunch. Lowell became a mecca for foreign visitors who marveled at how well the workers fared. The novelist Charles Dickens, for one, considered the Lowell factories a decided improvement over the "dark satanic mills" he knew at home. The Lowell girls, he wrote, wore "serviceable bonnets, good warm cloaks and shawls . . . , [were] healthy in appearance . . . , [and had] the manners and deportment of young women, not of degraded brutes."

Female factory workers line up in proper rows on their way to work.

tried to prevent its export to foreign countries—not un-like the way modern nations try to control the export of nuclear weapon technology, and with about as much success. In 1790 an English mechanic, Samuel Slater, with plans of the new English textile machinery in his head, arrived in the United States and established a cotton spinning factory at Pawtucket, Rhode Island. Before long southern New England was speckled with cotton yarn factories using Slater's water-driven machines and employing whole families to tend them. Francis Cabot Lowell, a generation later, visited England and brought back in his retentive memory the essentials for building a power loom.

Pooling his resources with other New England merchants, Lowell formed the Boston Manufacturing Company and began turning out vast quantities of textiles from his complex on the Merrimack River in the town named for him.

FOREIGN POLICY IN THE ERA OF GOOD FEELINGS

While technology was improving life at home, Monroe spent his eight years as president engaged in efforts weighted toward foreign rather than domestic policy. The president had been secretary of state and he found international affairs more engaging than contentious politicking in which domestic affairs were steeped.

His earliest accomplishments were two treaties with Great Britain. The Rush-Bagot Agreement of 1817 established mutual disarmament of the Great Lakes region and was the prelude to an eventual complete demilitarization of the U.S.-Canadian border, setting the stage for easy invasion of Buffalo, New York in the late twentieth century by clothes-mad Canadian shoppers. The Convention of 1818 extended the border with Canada along the 49th parallel from the Lake of the Woods to the crest of the Rockies. In the vaguely defined Oregon country beyond that point, there would be a joint British-American occupation for ten years. (In 1827, the Oregon arrangement was extended indefinitely, subject to one year's notice of termination, until the final disposition of the region could be decided.)

For many years, the acquisition of Spanish-controlled Florida had been a major goal of American policy. The U.S. came up with an elegant solution: We claimed we already owned it! In 1810, over the protest of the Spanish authorities, the U.S.A. simply annexed West Florida on the grounds that it had been a part of the Louisiana Territory purchased from France. The larger East Florida proved a problem more difficult to solve. It had become a source of friction as a haven for hostile Seminole Indians and runaway slaves, not to mention Poodle-eating Alligators. With the exception of the latter, the Washington authorities charged that the aforementioned groups threatened the safety of Americans in Georgia. In 1818 Andrew Jackson, commanding American troops along the border, crossed into Florida, hung two Britons accused of stirring up trouble, and seized the Spanish royal archives. Spain protested, but couldn't do much about it.

In 1819, Spain and America negotiated a wide-ranging agreement, the Adams-Onis Treaty, under which Spain renounced all claims to West Florida and ceded East Florida to the U.S. in exchange for its assuming claims by its citizens against Spain of $5 million. In addition, the treaty defined the western boundary of the Louisiana Territory by excluding Texas. And finally, Spain surrendered all claims to the Oregon country, leaving the U.S. and Britain to decide who owned it.

THE MONROE DOCTRINE

The Monroe Doctrine has something in common with the Industrial Revolution: Almost everyone had to write an essay on it at some point in high school. When Spain sold Florida to the U.S. for $5 million, it was being accommodating in part because it was besieged. Also, the strict matrons of Spanish society could never have tolerated the wet T-shirt contests found at Daytona Beach during Spring break. Weakened by the wars of the Napoleonic era, Spain lost control of its vast American empire and by 1820-21 virtually all its colonies had achieved their independence. Americans, sympathizing with the freedom struggles of the Latin American peoples, also welcomed the expulsion of European influence from the Western Hemisphere.

But would Europe stay out of American affairs? After 1815 the European nations established the Holy Alliance dedicated to maintaining the political status quo everywhere and resisting all revolutionary change. Americans feared that the European powers would now seek to restore reactionary Spanish rule in the region south of the United States. They also worried about recent moves by the Russians to extend their authority on the Pacific Coast from Alaska southward.

Britain too, for commercial reasons and because it feared French designs on Latin America, opposed Spain's regaining control of its former colonies. The American government declined a joint declaration with Britain, but Monroe included a statement about Latin America in his annual message of December 1823 promising resistance to any attempt by European powers "to extend their system to any portion of this hemisphere." At the same time, he stated, the United States had no interest in participating in Europe's wars or interfering with existing European colonies in the Western Hemisphere.

European leaders who bothered even to notice the Monroe Doctrine, as it came to be known, laughed at the presumption of the primitive North American republic. But the assertion established an important precedent. After mid-century, when American power and influence had expanded far beyond that of 1823, it confirmed the United States as a guarantor of Latin American freedom, whether Latin America wanted this help or not. Unfortunately, it also served over the years as an excuse for self-seeking American intervention in the internal affairs of its weaker Latin neighbors.

THE SECOND PARTY SYSTEM

Henry Clay (1777–1852).

The election of 1824 pitted Jackson against Clay, John Quincy Adams, and William Crawford of Georgia. No one received either a popular or electoral majority—though Jackson was first in both—and the election was thrown into the House of Representatives. Eventually the House chose Adams, and Jackson's partisans blamed Clay for siding with the secretary of state. When the new president chose Clay as his secretary of state there seemed no doubt that the two men had struck a "corrupt bargain."

The election of 1824 marked the beginning of "the second party system." Clay and Adams, whose party became known as the Whigs, had support among industrial areas in the North, while Jackson, from the party of the Democratic Republicans, later shortened to Democratic, found friends among small farmers of the South and West.

The election of 1828 brought Jackson and his party to power. The campaign was scandalous. The lack of TV journalists looking for a good sound bite didn't prevent Jackson from attacking Adams as a pimp, an extravagant aristocrat, and the perpetrator of the "corrupt bargain" in 1825. Adams got right down in the mud with him, asserting, among other unpleasant things, that Rachel Jackson had forgotten to divorce her first husband before marrying Andrew. Makes Clinton's "Gennifer-gate" look like a kiss from your sister. Voter turnouts were large, Jackson triumphed, and the nation entered a new political age.

THE JACKSONIAN REVOLUTION

Andrew Jackson was both symbol and agent of major changes on American political culture. Jackson himself was a prosperous slave holder whose estate near Nashville was a stately Old South "show plantation." He was also a leathery self-made man with minimal education and Quayle-like spelling ability who refused to acknowledge distinctions of rank and privilege. Despite his personal wealth, he brought to national politics a new egalitarian spirit that many of his political detractors found vulgar, coarse, and dangerous.

But Jackson was the beneficiary as well as instrument of political transformation. During the years following 1815 there had been a steady broadening of suffrage in the states, especially in the new states of the West. At the same time, state constitutions shifted the choice of presidential electors from the legislatures to the voters, thus moving the country closer to a government that was truly "by the people." The advent of the nominating

OLD HICKORY COMES TO WASHINGTON

Inauguration day, March 4, 1829. The city of Washington is full of strangers, many wearing homespun and coonskin caps and speaking in Irish brogues. The "people" are in town to see their hero anointed president. "I never saw anything like it," wrote the new senator from Massachusetts, Daniel Webster. "They really seem to think the country is rescued from some dreadful danger." Later, after Old Hickory took the oath of office, he invited his pals over to the White House. The crush was overwhelming, more and more people crowding in to get a glimpse of their hero. Finally some genius had an idea. Several kegs of whiskey were placed on the White House lawn, and half the crowd rushed outside. In today's temperate times, a local TV news station seeking man-on-the-street sound bites would probably do the trick.

convention to replace the party caucus, meanwhile, added a popular feature to the candidate-nomination process, and opened vast new markets for balloon, confetti, and funny hat manufacturers. What's more, the conventions would serve as a form of welfare for atonal amateur brass bands. From 1832 on all parties used the political convention to choose their nominees.

Jackson opposed economic privilege, supported laissez faire, and deplored the Whig policy of federal aid to business and enterprise. The chief target of Jackson's egalitarian wrath was the Second Bank of the United States, the "monster bank" that epitomized the vile marriage of government and economic privilege.

THE BIG BAD MONSTER BANK

In 1829 the Bank of the United States was the country's largest financial institution by far, and one of the most successful under its president, Nicholas Biddle, a haughty Philadelphia aristocrat. With branches all over the country, the BUS issued much of the country's paper money and kept it redeemable in gold. It also competed with state chartered banks in making loans to merchants, providing foreign exchange, and performing other business services. Finally, the BUS functioned as a modern central bank, providing extra currency and credit in hard times and tightening the supply of money and credit whenever necessary to hold down speculation and inflation.

However useful, it had made a host of enemies. Many of the state bankers believed its conservative "sound money" policies diminished their profits. In the West, businessmen and promoters often blamed the Bank's policies for holding back economic growth.

More than that, many Americans considered large corporations dangerous to democratic society. A mountain of capital as large as the BUS's was an invitation to corruption in government. And in truth, the BUS had a number of prominent politicians, including Clay and Daniel Webster, on permanent retainer, a connection that compromised their objectivity.

In 1832, with four years still left on its charter, its friends pushed through Congress an early re-charter bill to ensure continuity. On July 10 Jackson vetoed it with a scorching attack. In the election that year, Jackson won a thumping majority over both his adversaries and took his victory as a referendum against the Bank. To hasten the Bank's demise, he removed the government's deposits from it, and distributed them among favored state "pet banks," a move that will surely be replayed in a show titled "Banking's Biggest Bloopers," should Fox television ever find itself scraping for material.

The death of the BUS proved expensive for the nation. The government pet bank deposits fueled an economic boom, especially in the West, but the expansion alarmed the treasury which announced in July 1836 that it would accept only gold and silver for public lands. This pricked the bubble. Just as Jackson was leaving office a financial panic hit the nation ushering in hard times under the presidency of Martin Van Buren, who was defeated after one term by William Henry Harrison, the conqueror of Tecumseh, in 1840.

THE WHIGS ATTAIN POWER

THE VERY MODEL OF A MODERN MAJOR POLITICAL CAMPAIGN

The Whigs ran a very modern campaign against Van Buren, complete with floats, placards, campaign hats, emblems, parades, bonfires, huge rallies, and catchy slogans ("Tippecanoe and Tyler Too") that concealed the fact that they didn't have much of a program. Like certain present-day politicians, ex-general William Henry Harrison, a hero of the battle at Tippecanoe, was advised to keep his mouth shut lest he offend voters. He followed the advice, and with his running mate John Tyler (a states' rights Democrat from Virginia) won in a huge voter turnout.

WHIGS AND DEMOCRATS, NORTH AND SOUTH

Two new parties now expressed the fundamental division of the early republic between those who favored an activist federal government to encourage economic growth (the Whigs) and those who favored a limited federal government that would respect states' rights, keep its hands off the economy, and rely on private enterprise for prosperity (the Democrats). The division would continue until slavery shattered the political process and produced another major party readjustment. By the 1840s, the division between North and South that had long characterized America had become set in stone.

SUMMARY

By 1820, when Monroe ran without opposition, the nation's "first party" system had run its course. The Federalists were finished as a political party.

The Missouri Compromise—assuring a slave state would enter the Union each time a free state entered—would preserve sectional peace, but at the price of future danger to the Union.

Monroe's presidency was more successful in foreign affairs than in domestic, settling issues of the Canadian border and the ownership of Florida, and proclaiming the Monroe Doctrine concerning America's position toward European intervention in the Western Hemisphere.

The election of 1824 marked the beginning of "the second party system." Whigs under Clay and Adams had support among industrial areas in the North, while Jackson, from the party of the Democratic Republicans, later shortened to Democratic, found their supporters in the South.

CHAPTER 6

MANIFEST DESTINY:

SECTIONALISM AND WESTWARD EXPANSION

YOU MUST REMEMBER THIS

America's Manifest Destiny—the vast expansion of the nation toward the West—had a price: more or less continuous war first with Britain, then with the Indian tribes and Mexico. The antebellum period saw the birth of the two-party system, the creation of the modern political campaign, and the beginnings of an ominous division of the nation along fault lines both geographical and ideological.

IMPORTANT EVENTS

★ Texas declares independence, 1836
★ James K. Polk elected president, 1844
★ The Mexican War begins, 1846
★ The Wilmot Proviso, 1846
★ Peace Treaty with Mexico, 1848
★ The Seneca Falls Convention, 1848

Americans North and South shared values and goals derived from common experiences, but increasingly they came to think of themselves as members of separate societies with distinctive institutions and values. As time passed, these differences would burst the walls of mutual toleration and spark irreconcilable sectional resentments and grievances.

THE NORTH

The pre-Civil War North was a heterogeneous and volatile society, humming with enterprise and bursting with change. Most of its people were still farmers but the center of agriculture had shifted to the West, where many Northerners had moved, bringing their institutions, including their distaste for slavery, with them.

By 1860 almost all of the nation's modern industry, many of its most powerful banks, its largest corporations, and most of its shipping firms were located in New England and the Mid-Atlantic states.

WESTWARD MIGRATION

New lands in the West and generous federal land policies made possible the survival of the small farmer class. After the Land Ordinance of 1785 a succession of federal land laws had moved toward smaller minimal purchases at lower prices and even sales on credit. In 1830 the Preemption Act allowed squatters to take up 160 acres of public land at the minimum price of $1.25 an acre—another real estate bargain in a class with buying Manhattan from the Indians and Louisiana from the French. The Graduation Act of 1854 had nothing to do with education—it provided for a downward sliding scale for all unsold land that had remained on the market for ten

WHO'S
H
O
☛

Do These Names Ring a Bell?

🐝 **Martin Van Buren** (1782-1862).
Eighth president of the United States. Secretary of state under Jackson, elected president by a bare majority in 1836, then overwhelmingly defeated in 1840.

🐝 **William Henry Harrison** (1773-1841).
Ninth president of the United States. A famous soldier, defeated Tecumseh at Tippecanoe in 1811. Elected president in 1840 and died one month after his inauguration.

🐝 **John Tyler** (1790-1862).
Became tenth president of the United States upon Harrison's death in 1841.

🐝 **James K. Polk** (1795-1849).
Eleventh president of the United States. Congressman, and governor of Tennessee, he was elected president in 1844.

🐝 **William Lloyd Garrison** (1805-1879).
Journalist and antislavery campaigner. Editor of *The Liberator*, an abolitionist newspaper. After the abolition of slavery, he agitated for women's rights and the rights of American Indians.

🐝 **Elizabeth Cady Stanton** (1815-1902).
Social reformer and women's suffrage leader. Helped organize the first women's rights convention at Seneca Falls, NY, in 1848.

**WHO'S
H
O** ☞

(*continued*)

✎ **Lucretia Mott** (1793-1880).
Feminist, reformer, campaigner for peace, women's rights, and temperance. With Stanton, organized the 1848 Seneca Falls Convention.

✎ **Sam Houston** (1793-1863).
Soldier and statesman, congressman, governor of Tennessee, served in Mexican War, defeating the Mexicans at San Jacinto. Elected governor of Texas in 1859, but opposed secession from the Union and was deposed in 1861.

✎ **David Wilmot** (1814-1868).
Democratic congressman 1845-1851. Offered the Wilmot Proviso which would have prevented the extension of slavery into the territories.

years or more. But Westerners and the small farmer class wanted cheaper land still. During the 1850s their spokesmen demanded "homestead" legislation that would provide a completely free farm on the public domain for any head of family who honestly intended to cultivate it.

Easterners were not always happy with generous land laws. In the Northeast, pessimists feared the region's labor force would disappear as landless men rushed off to Ohio and Illinois to carve out farms. In the Southeast leaders claimed that cheap land would inevitably favor the free states. Ordinary folk from both sections, no fools, voted for cheap land with their feet. Unable to afford land at home, or to compete with the more fertile fields across the mountains, they packed up and set out for the virgin lands of the West.

Western settlement tended to follow lines of latitude. New Englanders moved to the regions just south of the Great Lakes, putting down roots in central and western New York and northern Ohio, Indiana, and Illinois and southern Michigan. Their new communities often reflected their old: compact settlement, puritan values, and respect for education and hard work. People from New York, New Jersey, and Pennsylvania overlapped the Yankees to some extent, but generally located in western regions a little further south. Many Southerners left the South entirely and settled in southern Ohio, Indiana, and Illinois where they farmed without slave labor. Many more moved to the newly developing slave states of the Southwest often carrying their slaves with them.

BEHIND THE SCENES

Little-Known Players and Unsung Heroes

People, few of them white males, who don't always make it into the history books.

Emma Willard (1787-1870).
Founder of the Troy Female Seminary, the first institution of higher learning for women in America.

Mary Lyon (1797-1849).
Founder of Mt. Holyoke College, the first women's college in the United States.

Pauline Wright Davis (1813-1876).
First American woman to use a model of the

BEHIND THE SCENES

(*continued*)

female anatomy while lecturing on physiology, and the founder in 1853 of Una, the first American newspaper devoted primarily to women's rights.

Maria Mitchell (1818-1889).
The first American woman astronomer, the discoverer of Mitchell's Comet (1847) and the first woman elected to the American Academy of Arts and Sciences (1848).

George Bancroft (1800-1891).
Secretary of the navy and minister to Great Britain in the Polk administration, he was most famous as a historian and the author of the 10-volume *History of the United States*, the first detailed historical account (in an era before the term "multicultural" even existed) of America from the founding of the colonies to the end of the Revolution.

Horace Mann (1796-1859).
Secretary of the State Board of Education in Massachusetts, a great crusader for free and universal public education. He served in Congress as a strong proponent of abolitionism, and ended his career as the first president of Antioch College.

Thomas Dorr (1805-1854).
A lawyer from a well-to-do family, Door led a violent rebellion in Rhode Island in 1842, protesting the state law that gave the vote only to holders of property.

By the 1840s this migration of thousands from the Atlantic coast had extended the division of the original states into free labor and slave labor regions all the way to the Missouri River.

WAGE EARNERS AND CITIES

The next largest component of free labor were the artisans, "mechanics," and operatives of the towns and cities. Many urbanites worked in the new factories springing up in the Northeast. In the New England textile mills many were young women. Other town dwellers worked as day laborers, digging, hauling, lifting, carrying, and receiving a wage of about a dollar a day. There was also a large servant class, predominantly female, that did the heavy household chores in the homes of the urban middle class.

WOMEN'S WORK

Harriet Beecher Stowe (1811–1896).

By the 1850s, a few women were business managers, running inns, shops, and schools. The era boasted a small class of women authors who made a mint writing sentimental stories and novels. The most eminent of the day was Harriet Beecher Stowe, member of a famous family of high achievers, whose 1852 antislavery novel *Uncle Tom's Cabin*—Abraham Lincoln believed—may have caused the Civil War! The growth and extension of public schools also created a new class of lady school teachers. There were few respectable jobs for educated unmarried women, and the school reformers of the day were able to tap a pool of cheap, competent labor among the era's middle class "spinsters."

The Northern town population also included many skilled workers: printers, mechanics, carpenters, blacksmiths, clerks, masons, cobblers, and others. These were almost entirely men and they were relatively well paid. Finally, there were the merchants, professionals, managers, industrialists, office holders, and assorted folk with "independent" incomes who made up the city and town elite.

IMMIGRANTS

From the mid-1840s until the Civil War immigration soared. By 1860, a large proportion of the North's unskilled labor force was foreign-born. These immigrants hailed from countries where poverty, famine, and political oppression made America look like a far better and safer place to live.

The European newcomers created a more diverse cultural and intellectual environment in the North, and a flood of new Irish and German immigrants made the Roman Catholic Church a force in American life for the first time. Not all Americans welcomed the new Catholic presence. Catholics were denounced for desecrating the Sabbath with sports, theater-going, picnicking, and other secular activities. They were attacked for being obedient to priests and to the church hierarchy.

Anti-Catholic and anti-foreign feelings took many forms. Some employers avoided hiring German or Irish workers—"No Irish need apply"—and some politicians demanded stricter immigration laws. Political battles developed between immigrants and Protestant Americans over the public schools and what they taught. In some cities Catholics and Catholic-owned property were physically assaulted and the authorities had to call out troops to restore order.

THE REFORM IMPULSE

The waves of Protestant religious revivalism that swept across America during this period, with their open air camp meetings and tub-thumping preachers, also gave life to new sects like Seventh Day Adventism and Mormonism. And the religious fervor was accompanied by a new zeal to remake society. Everywhere across the northern tier of the United States reformers began to address social ills. In Massachusetts Dorothea Dix took up the cause of the mentally ill, of prisoners, and of other occupants of public institutions. Also in Massachusetts, Horace Mann revitalized a decaying public school system, establishing many state supported high schools, a new curriculum, and the first teachers' training schools in the United States. In Maine Neal Dow became a crusader against family-destroying demon rum and induced the Maine legislature to adopt (1857) the first prohibition law.

ABOLITIONISM AND
WOMEN'S RIGHTS

Antislavery and the women's rights movement were among the most important of the ante-bellum causes. In Massachusetts William Lloyd Garrison fought for abolition in the 1830s. Several times the firebrand editor had to be rescued from mobs threatening to lynch him. Still, under more moderate leaders, the antislavery movement spread throughout the North, especially in New England.

The women's rights movement sprang from the crusade against slavery. American women were by law dependents of their fathers, or husbands, or brothers, and had few rights over their property or even their children. By the 1830s a few women were able to break out of the dependent mold by becoming teachers, authors, and editors, but it was still assumed that women had a distinct sphere tied to the family and should confine their energies to their roles as wives and mothers.

Social reform created a new domain for intelligent, middle class women to exercise their powers. Women were active in the movement to send Protestant ministers to the West and abroad. They worked for temperance and to improve the lot of the poor, of prisoners, and of the insane. They were active in the peace movement founded by William Ladd and Elihu Burritt, and in the movement to "purify" the sexual morals of men and women.

Elizabeth Cady Stanton (1815–1902).

Among the favorite causes of Northern women was the abolition of slavery. The refusal of the antislavery leaders, except Garrison, to accept women as equals in the movement prodded Elizabeth Cady Stanton, Lucretia Mott, and Angelina and Sarah Grimké to launch the women's rights movement in the 1840s. Their early efforts came to a head at the Seneca Falls Convention of July 1848. There the delegates adopted a twelve point Declaration of Sentiments modeled after the Declaration of Independence. It indicted Man for subjugating women, demanded the end of woman's exclusion from trades, professions, and commerce, and denounced educational discrimination and unequal legal status. A controversial resolution opposed by Lucretia Mott barely passed: It demanded for women the sacred right of the elective franchise.

During the next generation the women's rights movement spread across the entire North gaining strength each year and winning victories, especially in the area

OF BRAS AND BLOOMERS

Remember bra burning in the early 1970s? It wasn't the first time that clothes became a distraction from the real aims of the women's rights movement. During the 1850s, feminists adopted a skirt and pants combination that was supposed to preserve modesty while allowing freedom of movement. It became known as the "bloomer" after Amelia Bloomer, a newspaper editor in upstate New York. But feminists soon realized that it was distracting too much attention from more serious pursuits, and they gave it up except for sports.

of married women's rights over property and over their children after divorce.

One part of the pre-Civil War social ferment went beyond reform and rejected all of the North's bustling commercial, individualistic society in favor of small communities based on cooperation and social justice. Communitarians' schemes invariably were founded on the view that human nature was fundamentally benign and generous. Some of these social experiments—the Shaker

A Shaker religious service.

communities, Oneida, Etienne Cabet's Icaria, and others—were held together by a Christian ideal. Others, such as New Harmony, Brook Farm, and the Fourierist "Phalanxes" touted by newspaper publisher Horace Greeley, professed some sort of secular socialism. Almost all the secular communities failed in a few years. The religious ones generally lasted longer.

THE SOUTH

The South experienced little of this cultural ferment, becoming ever more self-protective and defensive of its slave system. While the South was not a uniform whole—its climate, soil, and crops varied widely—above all, there was cotton.

THE SOUTHERN ECONOMY

Cotton was by far the South's major cash crop, though its cultivation was confined to the warmest sections. In 1859 the major cotton growing states were, in order, Mississippi, Alabama, Louisiana, Georgia, Texas, Arkansas, and South Carolina. Cotton was raised on both large plantations and small farms, though plantations—units with twenty or more slaves—were far more productive per acre. Despite the venerable myths, planters were not impractical aristocrats uninterested in profits. On the contrary, they were often skilled businessmen who ran their estates on rational cost-effective lines with a closely supervised and highly efficient labor force. In some ways the cotton plantations were among the most efficient business units of the period. During the years just before the Civil War, the cotton growing region of the South had one of the highest per capita incomes in the United States.

SLAVERY

But if raising cotton produced comfort and abundance for white planters and farmers, it was very different for the black slaves. By 1860 there were 3.9 million slaves in the Old South, about one-third the total population, most of them in the cotton- and rice-growing regions. Not all blacks were slaves. In 1860, about a quarter of a million "free people of color" inhabited the South, most living in Maryland, Virginia, Kentucky, and Missouri, the so-called "border states."

The lives of slaves were not easy. Their work day was from dawn to dusk, with few breaks and little time for meals. Housing and food were poor compared with that enjoyed by free labor in the North. Discipline varied. Every Southern state forbade gratuitous cruelty toward slaves in its black code, but it was difficult to enforce these rules. And none of them prohibited physical punishment, including lashes well laid on, for disobedience to the master's will.

Most deplorable of all, however, were practices that deprived slaves of their humanity. Slaves were property and could be bought, sold, bequeathed, and inherited like other property. They had no freedom of movement and went when and where their masters determined. Slave families had no legal standing and masters could separate children from parents and parents from each other. Slaves could not be taught to read and write, though some learned nonetheless. Some slaves, favored by their owners, acquired skills and were even allowed to hire themselves out for pay, a part of which they could sometimes keep. But to be a slave in the Old South meant remaining a permanent child, a dependent, kept forever in subordination unless your owner freed you.

And yet the system did not destroy all hope or attainment. Most slaves were able to maintain a reasonable family life. They also developed a cultural and artistic life composed of African and European elements but transformed by the American experience. Slave music and a rich oral literature circulated in the slave quarters and even attracted the favorable attention of whites. Slaves also enjoyed the consolation of religion. Served predominantly by preachers of their own race, they adopted an emotional version of Christianity that provided an outlet for yearnings and filled a need for solace.

THE WHITE SOUTH

White society in the Old South was not a uniform whole. The planter class, though admired, envied, and heeded, was not large. Far more typical was the small farmer who owned some slaves but worked alongside them in the fields himself. No lordly mansion with white colonnades for such a man. Rather, he often lived in an enlarged cabin, frequently of logs, with three or four sparsely furnished, dirt-floored rooms. In the hilly or mountainous areas farmers owned few if any slaves, and many resented the power and arrogance of the planter class on the richer soils.

The South was overwhelmingly rural. Outside the border states, there was only one major city in the slave states, New Orleans. Most other places were little more than local political centers or small market towns without the social and cultural variety of larger communities.

Most Southerners considered cotton growing and other agricultural pursuits superior to Northern industry and commerce. They were profitable, they suited the Southern temperament, and they provided a degree of social stability that a slave society required, said Southern conservatives. In fact, in response to abolitionist criticism, Southern journalists and politicians argued that slave society was better for whites than free society and

GONE WITH THE WIND DOESN'T QUITE TELL THE WHOLE STORY.

Movies and novels leave the impression that the ante-bellum South consisted of slaves and slave owners living on huge plantations, and something called "po' whites"—white people who lived in poverty and couldn't afford to own slaves. In fact, most people in the South belonged to none of these groups. In 1860, fewer than 25% of the population belonged to slave holding families. Most of these owned ten slaves or less. Only 1% of families owned more than a hundred slaves. There were 250,000 free blacks in the South as well, mostly in the upper South—about half of them in Maryland and

Virginia. The largest group of Southerners were farmers who owned no slaves at all. Still, it was the few large planters who controlled the region's wealth and had the most influence on its politics.

Gone with the Wind (MGM, 1939) tells its own version of the Civil War and its ramifications in the American South.

kinder ultimately to all its members including the slaves themselves. By the 1840s the Old South was well on its way to becoming an intellectually closed society intent on preserving its special social system at all costs and willing to drive away all those who questioned its perfection.

And so by the eve of the Civil War, the United States was rapidly moving in the direction of two societies within one national boundary. North and South continued to be tied together by national political parties, national religious denominations, and by shared historical memories and trade connections. But these were weakening and would soon suffer an enormous shock beyond their ability to absorb.

"Settlers, Kemosabe, millions of 'em."

EXPANSIONISM

Despite the widening chasm of values, economic interest, culture, and institutions the two sections might have cohered if not for the issue of territorial expansion. In the 1840s the United States added 1 million square miles to its political area and the strains created enormous centripetal forces.

One addition was Oregon, a vast slab of territory running from northern California to Russian Alaska, over whose ownership some were willing to fight with Britain. Everyone remembers the slogan "54:40' or Fight," and now you can tell everyone whose it was: James K. Polk's, in the 1844 presidential campaign.

The bellicose feelings aroused by Oregon were part of an expansionist movement labeled Manifest Destiny that

WAR WITH CANADA?
. . . .
Yes, we did in a sense once go to war with our Friendly Neighbor to the North, though it was more like a continuation of our age-old disputes with Britain. Back in 1783, the British and American peace commissioners in Paris had used an inaccurate map to determine the Maine-Canada border, putting 7.5 million acres in dispute. The issue came to a head in 1842 when Maine residents and Canadians clashed over the fertile Aroostock Valley, precipitating a nasty little frontier war. Fortunately, both sides preferred peace: the Webster-Ashburton Treaty of 1842 saved the Aroostock Valley for the U.S., but gave Britain much of the disputed region. Later, more authentic maps were found that made it clear that the 1783 treaty had actually awarded much of the disputed land to the U.S., so we probably gave up more than we had to.

assigned Americans a God-given right to occupy the entire North American continent sweeping aside other territorial claims and replacing all native people and cultures. These views had become influential especially within the Democratic party and among Southerners and Westerners.

THE MEXICAN BORDERLANDS

While the Oregon pot simmered, American expansionists turned their attention to the Southwest. There the young Mexican Republic ruled over a vast territory bordering the United States, separated by miles of desert and mountains from the nation's capital of Mexico City.

The Mexican authorities in the city of Montezuma disagreed over policies for their nation's border lands— Texas, New Mexico, and California. The pro-American

---

MANIFEST DESTINY
. . . .

"Manifest Destiny" wasn't invented by a politician (or
his speech writer) but by a New York newspaperman,
John L. O'Sullivan, who wrote in 1845 that it was "the
fulfillment of our manifest destiny to overspread the
continent allotted by Providence for the free development of our yearly expanding millions." He had Texas
in mind, but the phrase soon came to be used in connection with Oregon and Alaska, and, yes, eventually to
justify early twentieth-century American empire-building.

Federalistas favored local autonomy for the separate Mexican states and encouraged settlement of the border regions to aid Mexican development. The anti-American
Centralistas favored tight control over all Mexican territory and opposed accelerated settlement of the outlying
regions, especially by foreigners.

TEXAS

Between 1823 and 1830, about 8,000 white Americans
and a thousand black slaves settled in Texas, mostly in
the southeastern region. They had been granted the
right to live there by the Federalistas under certain con-
ditions, including the acceptance of the Catholic faith.

But then the Centralistas came to power and the political climate for Americans in Texas drastically changed.
The Colonization Law of 1830 forbade citizens of foreign
countries lying adjacent to the Mexican territory to settle
in Texas and called for the garrisoning of Mexican
troops in the state of Coahuila-Texas to keep the Americans in line. Inevitably, the American settlers felt
threatened.

THE ALAMO, PRE-DISNEY

Things came to a head when General Santa Anna took power as a dictator in 1832. He headed north with an army of 6,000, intending to impose central rule on the Americans. In San Antonio he met a force of 187 Texans entrenched behind the walls of a former mission. The results were unhappy for the Texans (though quite satisfactory for Fess Parker, thank you very much), and "Remember the Alamo!" became a rallying cry for Texas independence. Sam Houston, a former governor of Tennessee was chosen by a group of Texans as commander-in-chief of their army in 1836, and he soon delivered a great victory at San Jacinto, capturing Santa Anna into the bargain. Santa Anna promised to grant Texas independence if given his freedom. Though he soon repudiated his pledge, never again would Mexico be able to impose its authority on the Texans.

In The Alamo *(United Artists, 1960), Hollywood sent John Wayne in to kick some Mexican butt in a Technicolor retelling of the 1836 massacre.*

The Lone Star Republic now began its ten-year history as an independent nation, with the U.S. officially recognizing it in March 1837. Most Texans wanted to be incorporated into the Union but some Americans feared it would lead to war with Mexico. Southerners anticipated with pleasure the very thing the Northern free-staters deplored: adding to the number of slave states. Advocates of Manifest Destiny also naturally favored annexation.

THE ALAMO: WHAT IS THIS PLACE, AND WHY ARE THERE SOLDIERS INSIDE?

The "Alamo Mission" was a chapel of the Franciscan Mission San Antonio de Valero founded in 1718. But the mission was abandoned when its regular customers—Indians—pretty much disappeared from the area. During the nineteenth century, it was periodically used as a fort. And so it was being used by Jim Bowie and Davy Crockett, along with a few dozen others, when Santa Anna headed north to civilize the Americans. The siege lasted 13 days, at the end of which the Mexicans overran the fort, killing all but five men. Santa Anna ordered those five killed after the fighting was over. The name Alamo comes from the Spanish word for the cottonwood trees among which the building stood.

The Alamo today.

THE MEXICAN WAR

Actual annexation waited until Polk's election victory in 1844. The Democrats called this a mandate for annexation and even before the new president's inauguration, Congress accepted Texas into the Union by a joint resolution of both houses by majority vote, far easier to achieve than the two-thirds of the Senate required by a treaty.

Mexico immediately broke diplomatic relations with the United States and sent troops north to the Texas border. But Mexican-American tensions went beyond mere annexation. The Texans claimed the Rio Grande as the southwestern boundary of the new state rather than the Nueces, a contention that added thousands of square miles to Texas at Mexico's expense. The Mexicans denied these claims. And then there was California, which Polk had tried to buy from Mexico (and no smart remarks about your wanting to sell it back to them today). It was filled with Americans and it seemed likely that, as in Texas, an American uprising would soon challenge Mexican rule.

Meanwhile Polk was trying to settle the Oregon issue with Great Britain. A Southerner, he preferred the sunny Southwest to cool and rainy Oregon and compromised by agreeing to extend the Canadian-American border to the Pacific along the 49th parallel (excepting Vancouver Island). There is no record of his having changed his slogan from 54:40' or Fight to 49:00' and Let's Be Happy We Got That Much, but Congress reluctantly went along with him.

FIGHTING IN MEXICO

On May 11 Polk delivered a war message to Congress proclaiming the legitimacy of U.S. territorial claims and citing a skirmish with the Mexicans near the Rio Grande that left eleven Americans dead and fifty captured. Congress declared war, appropriated $10 million to fight it, and approved a military force of 50,000 volunteers. Though the war declaration itself had been almost unanimous, 67 not entirely logical Whigs voted against the appropriation and the volunteer force.

Indeed, there would be widespread opposition to the war to the very end. Many Whigs considered it a Democratic war that served the interests of the opposition party. One of these Whig critics was a one-term congressman from Illinois named Abraham Lincoln. In the North, moreover, many judged the war a trick of the slave powers to add to the number of slave states. Still other opponents saw it as a brutal war of conquest against a weaker neighbor.

This map depicts Taylor's Campaign in Mexico,
1846–1847.

Yet the fighting itself went without a hitch. The first victories were scored by Zachary Taylor against the Mexican invaders at Palo Alto and Resaca de la Palma even before Congress had officially declared war. The craggy general became an instant hero known as Old Rough and Ready. Soon after, the Army of the West under

Stephen Kearny took Santa Fe, the New Mexico capital, and then pushed on overland to California.

Kearny and John C. Frémont fought in California, eventually defeating the weak forces the Mexicans could muster there. Meanwhile, the Americans advanced against the main enemy centers in Mexico itself from two directions. Taylor's forces attacked across the Rio Grande and in a series of engagements culminating in the Battle of Buena Vista (February 1847) defeated Santa Anna convincingly. The decisive blow was delivered by Winfield Scott's campaign against Mexico City launched from Vera Cruz on the Atlantic.

In early March 1847 Scott's army landed at Vera Cruz on the Gulf of Mexico. Three weeks later, the city surrendered and Scott began the ascent from the steamy coast to the cool central plateau where the Mexican capital was located and where Santa Anna had withdrawn his troops. The Americans remained outside awaiting the results of peace negotiations begun by Nicholas P. Trist, an American commissioner who accompanied Scott's army. But negotiations broke down, and on September 13, Scott entered Mexico City. Soon after, Santa Anna was deposed by the Mexicans and fled the country.

PEACE—AND GRABBING SOME REAL ESTATE

Peace was formalized by the Treaty of Guadalupe Hidalgo signed in February 1848. Under its terms Mexico surrendered its claims to all of Texas including the disputed section. It also relinquished to the United States all of New Mexico and California. The vast Mexican Cession included parts, or all, of present-day California, Arizona, Nevada, Utah, Colorado, and Wyoming, and added almost 1.2 million square miles to the United States. In exchange the United States government paid Mexico

$15 million and assumed $3 million in American citizens' claims against the Mexican government.

For some, this was not enough, and the treaty was attacked by expansionists in the Senate as a bad bargain. We won, they felt, so why not take all of Mexico? In the end, fear of incorporating into the United States densely populated regions of non-Americans brought dissenters around, and the Senate ratified the treaty as signed by Trist and the Mexicans.

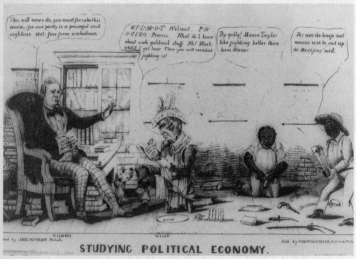

STUDYING POLITICAL ECONOMY.

One cartoonist's take on the Whigs, the Wilmot Proviso, and the Mexican War in 1848.

DAVID WILMOT: REMEMBERED ONLY FOR HIS PROVISO

It was indeed a glorious victory, but it also raised ominous questions. In August 1846, while the war was still new, a Democratic representative from Pennsylvania, David Wilmot, had introduced an amendment to an appropriation bill stipulating that any territory acquired from Mexico must be free of slavery. The Wilmot Proviso immediately became the eye of a stormy debate. Antislavery Northerners defended it with appeals to human rights and the rights of free white labor which, they said, would avoid any region where slavery was entrenched. Southerners, led by John C. Calhoun of South Carolina, insisted that the territories were owned by all the states alike. Common justice decreed that Southerners could bring their property, including slaves, into any part of them. The Proviso passed the House several times but never made it through the Senate. Yet it would not go away. Instead, it remained in the wings, ready to be invoked at moments of sectional friction. There would be many of these in the years just ahead.

SUMMARY

- The two party system—Whigs on one side of the aisle, Democrats on the other—was secure by 1840.

- The expansionist movement called Manifest Destiny was the impulse behind the Mexican War, the Indian Wars, and the threat to go to war with Britain over Oregon.

- The women's rights movement grew out of the antislavery crusade and flourished in the 1840s.

- The Wilmot Proviso—an amendment to an appropriations bill stipulating that any territory taken from Mexico must be free of slavery—never made it through the Senate, yet it remained as a constant reminder of sectional friction.

CHAPTER 7

FREE STATES AND SLAVE:
A HOUSE DIVIDING

YOU MUST REMEMBER THIS

The first generation to enjoy the fruits of freedom from British domination soon found new enemies within their own house. And among the myriad political and economic conflicts of the day, the issue that divided them more than any other, that pervaded public and private discourse, that profoundly influenced every political and many personal acts was the searing problem of slavery.

IMPORTANT EVENTS

- ★ *Uncle Tom's Cabin* published, 1851
- ★ The Kansas-Nebraska Act, 1854
- ★ The Dred Scott decision, 1857
- ★ The Lincoln-Douglas debates, 1858
- ★ John Brown executed for Treason, 1859
- ★ Lincoln elected president, 1860
- ★ Civil War begins at Fort Sumter, 1861

CALIFORNIA

The Whig party won its second, and last, presidential victory in 1848 with the ticket of Zachary Taylor (Old Rough and Ready) and Millard Fillmore, favorite of trivia buffs the world over. In March 1849, the new president found himself in a bitter struggle over the territories that would persist until the final crisis of the Union.

With the divisive issue of slavery dominating the nation's public life, the new president, Zachary Taylor, recommended that Congress admit California under its free

---

GOLD!

In early 1848, an employee of the Swiss entrepreneur Johann Augustus Sutter found gold in the foothills of the Sierra Nevada mountains. Sutter tried to keep the discovery quiet but failed and in weeks a wild rush to the gold diggings had gathered irresistible momentum. Overland by wagon, by ship around Cape Horn, by ship and railroad to and through Panama, thousands descended on northern California to share in the wealth that suddenly seemed there for the taking. Most failed miserably and returned home richer only in experience. Others stayed. By late 1849 the territory had 100,000 inhabitants, sojourners, and permanent residents.

CALIFORNIA, 1849   CALIFORNIA, TODAY

WHO'S HO ☛

Do These Names Ring a Bell?

Zachary Taylor (1784-1850).
Twelfth president of the United States. General and Indian fighter, Whig candidate in 1848. He favored admission of California as a slave state. His son-in-law was Jefferson Davis.

John Brown (1800-1859).
Abolitionist who wandered the country pursuing his cause. His ill-thought-out attack on the Federal arsenal at Harpers Ferry led to his conviction for murder and treason. He was hanged in 1859.

Daniel Webster (1782-1852).
Lawyer, orator, statesman. Declined presidential nomination by Whigs in 1844. Secretary of state under W.H. Harrison, and again under Fillmore.

Millard Fillmore (1800-1874).
Thirteenth president of the United States, 1850-54.

Franklin Pierce (1804-1869).
Fourteenth president of the United States, 1854-58. Brigadier general in Mexican War, he defended slavery and the fugitive slave law.

James Buchanan (1791-1868).
Fifteenth president of the United States, secretary of state under Polk. Elected president in 1856. Strongly favored maintenance of slavery and establishment of Kansas as a slave state.

state constitution and organize Utah and New Mexico as territories without reference to slavery. The South clung to its equality in the upper house and denounced the president's plan. Afraid to upset the exact balance of free and slave states in the Senate, Congress balked.

SECTIONAL RESENTMENTS

North-South issues went beyond the delicate Senate balance. Southerners resented Northern efforts, exemplified by the Wilmot Proviso, to exclude slavery from the territories. These lands, they said, were the common property of all sections and Southerners must have the same rights in them, including the right to hold slave property, as other Americans. Most believed that only when a territory entered the Union as a state could it exclude slavery. Neither the people of a territory, nor Congress could make that decision any sooner.

Southerners also resented deeply the Northern anti-slavery agitation. Admittedly, not every Northerner was an abolitionist, but increasingly, they said, Northerners were closing ranks against further expansion of slavery. In 1848, besides the Whig and Democratic tickets, there had been a third party in the field, the Free Soil party, dedicated to preserving the Mexican Cession for "free labor." Its candidate, former president Martin Van Buren, had won only 300,000 votes out of 2.9 million cast, but the new political alignment marked growing Northern hostility to Dixie and seemed, to Southerners, a harbinger of emerging Northern intransigence.

There also was the Northern attitude toward runaway slaves. Yankees seemed determined to empty the South of slaves. They aided runaways through the "underground railroad," a chain of safe houses leading north to Canada whence slaves would not be extradited to the

United States. They also impeded efforts by Southerners to recover fugitive slaves. Though federal law explicitly authorized slave owners to recapture slaves who fled to the free states, Northern legislatures, through "personal liberty laws," often blocked recovery of fugitives. Perhaps only a thousand slaves escaped from the South each year, still many Southerners considered Northern attitudes an outrageous violation of a sectional obligation enjoined by the Constitution.

Northern grievances were the mirror-image of the Southerners'. Though the South was the minority section, Yankees charged, it wielded disproportionate in-

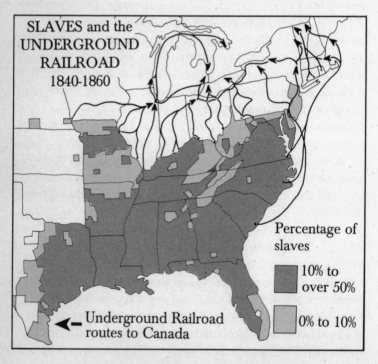

SLAVES and the
UNDERGROUND
RAILROAD
1840-1860

Percentage of slaves

10% to over 50%

0% to 10%

◄— Underground Railroad routes to Canada

This map depicts routes used by Southern blacks to escape slavery, 1840–1860.

fluence on the nation's affairs. Southerners controlled
the Democratic party, the more successful of the two
parties, and through this control dominated national
policy. Southern interests had overridden those of the
North in preventing passage of bills for rivers and harbor
improvements, for homestead legislation to provide free
farms in the West, for a protective tariff, and for a Pacific
railroad by way of a central or northern route. As for
fugitive slaves, they were at the very least entitled to constitutional protection until their runaway status was
proven. The South's indifference to such rights was a
measure of its priorities: its property rights in slaves were
of major importance.

The most incendiary North-South clash, however, was
over the status of slavery in the territories. Few Northerners doubted that Congress had the clear authority to
exclude slavery from the territories; it had done so without serious challenge ever since the Northwest Ordinance of 1787. Many also believed that it should use this
power without delay, for once slavery entered a federal
territory, then free labor would avoid it.

Southerners were uncertain whether Congress had the
legal right to bar slavery from the federal territories. But
if it had the power, it must not use it. Southerners, like
Northerners, had paid for the territories in cash and
blood and had the same right as other Americans to
bring their property to the new regions.

These attitudes and issues became the center of a ran-
corous debate as Congress took up the question of California statehood. Members were so divided by section
that fist fights between Yankees and Southerners broke
out on the House floor. Outside Congress, meanwhile,
a group of Southern fire-eaters (partisans prone to in-
flammatory speeches) scheduled a convention in Nashville to consider the possibility of secession from the
Union if Southern territorial demands were not met.

BEHIND THE SCENES

Little-Known Players and Unsung Heroes

People, few of them white males, who don't always make it into the history books.

Elizabeth Blackwell (1821-1910).
The first woman to graduate from an American medical school (1849), she later founded the New York Infirmary.

Margaret Fuller (1810-1850).
Probably the most powerful intellect among nineteenth-century feminists, author of *Woman in the 19th Century*.

Hinton Rowan Helper (1829-1909).
A Southerner, and the author of *The Impending Crisis of the South*, a book arguing that slavery was weakening the economy of the South as well as the structure of Southern society. The Republicans used its ideas effectively in the 1860 election.

Dred Scott (c. 1795-1858).
The Supreme Court ruled against his contention that he was a free man because he lived in a free state, but he was soon emancipated and lived out his days as a hotel porter in St. Louis.

Henry Highland Garnet (1815-1882).
One of the most famous American abolitionists, he was born on a slave plantation in Maryland. He studied at Oneida Theological Seminary in New York.

THE COMPROMISE OF 1850

The center of debate in the Senate was a cluster of proposals by the elder statesman from Kentucky, Henry Clay, a man who had built his career on compromise and love of the Union. Clay's scheme was designed to settle outstanding sectional differences by a series of tradeoffs: California would be admitted to the Union as a free state; the rest of the Mexican Cession would be organized into territories without mention of slavery; Texas would surrender its boundary claims to New Mexico, but its public debts would be assumed by the federal government; the slave trade in the District of Columbia would be abolished, but the legality of slavery in the District would be confirmed; Congress would pledge never to interfere with the interstate slave trade and it would pass an airtight fugitive slave act.

Daniel Webster (1782–1852). Famous orator, strong Unionist, notorious compromiser on the subject of slavery.

The Clay measures won the support of Daniel Webster and other strong Unionists, but were bitterly opposed by the dying Calhoun who sat as a colleague read his speech denouncing the North for refusing the South its sacred rights. Also opposed, though from the other side, were two champions of free soil, Senators William Seward of New York and Salmon Chase of Ohio. Seward called the Clay scheme "radically wrong and essentially vicious" and proclaimed that even the Constitution could not protect slavery for there "was a higher law," the law of God, under which all men are free.

In the Compromise of 1850, a patchwork of solutions that satisfied nobody was used to cover over disagreements about the status of slavery in California, New

Mexico, Utah, and the District of Columbia. The Fugitive Slave Law of 1850 required free citizens to aid federal slave-catchers on pain of fine and jail sentence. When the first federal commissioners came north in pursuit of runaways many communities resisted, sometimes violently.

In May, 1854 slave catchers pursued the Virginia slave, Anthony Burns, to Boston and despite excited mass rallies and an attempt by abolitionists to recapture him, carried him back to Virginia under guard by armed federal soldiers. Incidents such as Burns' "rendition" made many instant Northern converts to the antislavery cause. One conservative Bostonian remarked of the Burns affair that he had gone "to bed one night an old fashioned, conservative, compromise Union Whig and waked up a stark mad abolitionist."

HARRIET BEECHER STOWE

One Northerner stirred to outrage over slavery was the wife of a professor of religion at Bowdoin College in Maine, Harriet Beecher Stowe. In 1851 Mrs. Stowe began a series of sketches for an antislavery newspaper dealing with Southerners, white and black, caught in the web of slavery. Published in book form as a novel, *Uncle Tom's Cabin* became a raging bestseller and converted thousands to ardent antislavery.

Introduced as a single bill, the Clay proposals were defeated, but the Democratic senator from Illinois, Stephen A. Douglas, reintroduced them as separate bills. This time, Taylor, who had opposed the compromise, had died, and his successor Fillmore favored a sectional accommodation. A modified version of the Clay compromise passed, a set of five bills that have come to be called the Compromise of 1850.

BUM RAP FOR FILLMORE?

The mere mention of Millard Fillmore's name brings on snickers—he's everyone's model of ineffectuality. But hold on a second. Fillmore was apprenticed to a fuller and clothier as a youth (to full is to shrink and thicken wool, as you surely know), he taught himself law, ran a highly successful law partnership in upstate New York, became a member of Congress and eventually chairman of the House Ways and Means Committee. He was a forward thinking proponent of the high-tech of his day, carrying through, against strong opposition, a $30,000 appropriation to subsidize Morse's telegraph. He opposed the annexation of Texas as a slave state, favored excluding slavery from the District of Columbia, and opposed slave trade between the states. He became vice-president in 1848, then took over as president after Taylor's death in 1850. His signing of the Fugitive Slave Law cost him popularity in the North, and the Whigs refused to renominate him in 1852. He did run, however, as a candidate of the American (Know-Nothing) party, carrying only one state, Maryland. OK, so he's not Lincoln or FDR, but without trying too hard we could probably name a dozen or so other presidents with less interesting or admirable careers.

California would be admitted as a free state; New Mexico and Utah would be organized as territories, both to decide for or against slavery only at the time of admission as states; the disputed Texas-New Mexico boundary would be adjusted in favor of New Mexico; the slave trade in the District of Columbia would be prohibited; and there would be a new, more stringent law to guarantee the return of fugitive slaves. In other words, bitter opponents created a gerry-built structure of laws that did not address the fundamental source of their disagreement.

"SLAVE POWER" EXPANSIONISM

Southerners could see that however the sectional issue in the territories was resolved, most of the remaining undeveloped regions of the United States were not congenial to slavery. But what about the lands and islands to the South? Here, in the warmth of Central America and the Caribbean, American slavery and slave society might flourish, and through new colonies or even new states, the South might offset its loss of power elsewhere to the North.

During the 1850s, Southern expansionists pushed for acquiring more territory from Mexico and in 1853 secured a strip of land along the Southern U.S. boundary for $10 million (the Gadsden Purchase). The same drive incited raids by Americans across the U.S.-Mexico border and several attempts by Tennesseean William Walker, the "gray-eyed man of destiny," to seize control of Nicaragua and set himself up as ruler.

CUBA LOOKS NICE, TOO. WE'LL TAKE IT.

But Southerners most coveted Cuba, a rich Spanish colony with slave-run sugar plantations only ninety miles off Florida. In 1848, the Polk administration offered Spain $100 million for it, and when Spain refused, Southern adventurers tried to foment revolution among discontented Cubans in hope of eventually annexing the country. In 1854 the Pierce administration instructed Pierre Soulé, U.S. minister to Spain, to offer $130 million to the Spanish government, and, if Spain refused, to direct his attention to the forcible separation of the island from Spain. Spain refused again, and Soulé met with the American ministers to Paris and London to consider the next move. In a memorandum to Washington, he declared Cuba "necessary to the North American republic," and announced that "by every law, human and Divine, we shall be justified in wresting it from Spain." This "Ostend Manifesto," leaked to the press, was denounced by many Northerners as another example of the outrageous imperialist appetite of the Southern "slave power." Thus President Kennedy was not the first U.S. leader to botch an assault on America's island neighbor.

AND CUBA WASN'T THE ONLY THING WE WERE SHOPPING FOR

In 1853, the U.S. went shopping in Mexico again, buying a strip of land which is now part of Arizona and New Mexico for $10 million. The U.S. felt this deal, called the Gadsden Purchase, was necessary for a projected railroad from New Orleans to the Pacific coast. We even tried to buy Lower California, but the Mexicans weren't selling, not even at the offering price of $50 million.

Kansas-Nebraska

Stephen Douglas (1813–1861).

The Ostend Manifesto affair erupted in the midst of another sectional dispute set off inadvertently by Stephen Douglas. An Illinois Democrat married to a slave-holding Southern heiress, Douglas took a pragmatic, rather than a moral, view of slavery. Slavery, he felt, was a fact of life, and must be accepted where it existed by state laws to preserve the Union. The best way to do this, he concluded, was through "popular sovereignty," whereby people in the territories themselves, prior to statehood, could accept or reject slavery without congressional intervention. Popular sovereignty appealed to the democratic instincts of the American people while at the same time it promised to remove the slave extension issue from the congressional stage where it served as a continuous sectional incitement.

LET'S MAKE A DEAL, STARRING STEPHEN DOUGLAS

As head of the Senate Committee on Territories and a promoter of his home city of Chicago, Douglas was interested in western development and a Pacific railroad by a central route. From this modest aim he unleashed a juggernaut of vitriolic debate and intense politicking, the musty details of which are as follows: In January 1854 he introduced a bill to create Nebraska territory out of that part of the Louisiana Purchase territory closed to slavery under the Missouri Compromise. Providing the Nebraska country with the machinery of government would, he knew, accelerate its settlement and make the case for a central route Pacific railroad more attractive.

The bill, as it initially stood, promised one or more new free states in the plains and would further reduce Southern power in Congress. It would also virtually surround slave-state Missouri with a sea of free soil. To a group of powerful Southern senators, who lacked Douglas's concern for railroading, this outcome seemed intolerable. They told Douglas that he could forget about his bill unless it allowed Southern settlers to bring their "species of property" (their euphemism for slaves) to the new territory. In response, Douglas inserted into the bill a popular sovereignty proviso; the Missouri Compromise notwithstanding, the people of the territory might decide the slavery issue for themselves. When this did not satisfy the Southern solons, he bent over backwards again (could he touch the floor yet?), adding to the bill the explicit repeal of the Missouri Compromise. Pushed hard by the Southerners in Congress, by the Douglas Democrats, and by the Pierce administration, the bill passed in May 1854 as the Kansas-Nebraska Act after three months of angry debate.

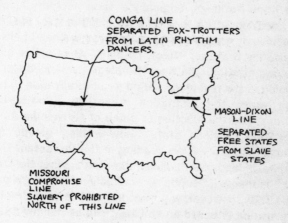

THE REPUBLICAN PARTY

The Kansas-Nebraska Act jolted to life a new strictly sectional political Republican party dedicated to confining slavery within its existing limits. Of course, few Southerners supported the Republicans' platform of slavery exclusion from the national territories, but the party's beliefs did not win universal support in the North either. Many Yankees, especially Catholics, recent immigrants, and transplanted Southerners, remained solid for the Democrats. The new Republican party did best in the "upper north" where many voters were Protestant New Englanders or their descendants, and where New England institutions like public schools and temperance societies flourished.

THE RISE AND FALL OF THE
UNLAMENTED KNOW-NOTHINGS

For a time, it looked as if the successor to the Whigs, now fatally weakened by the deaths of Clay and Webster in 1852, might be the Americans, better known as the Know-Nothings, originally a secret society inspired by nativism. The name was inspired by the self-consciously mysterious habit its members had of always answering that they "knew nothing" when asked about the organization. The Know-Nothings demanded the extension of the residence period for naturalization to fourteen years, the restriction of voting to native-born citizens, and the election to office of native-born Americans only. Various state Know-Nothing groups also championed prohibition, reading of the Protestant Bible in schools, and other policies directed against the Catholic "menace." Despite spectacular election gains in the 1850s, however, it proved impossible to maintain a cohesive party based on nativism, and by the mid-1850s the Know-Nothings had begun to disintegrate into what we'll unofficially call the "Accomplished Littles."

BLEEDING KANSAS

The Republican party grew stronger as sectional antipathies worsened. Within weeks of passage of the Kansas-Nebraska Act the territory of Kansas—split off from Nebraska by a late version of the bill—became a ferocious battleground of slave-state and free-state settlers determined to impose their views on the new community.

There was violence and fraud on both sides. In the fall of 1854, 1,700 armed Missourians crossed into Kansas and illegally elected a pro-slavery territorial delegate to Congress. In early 1856 an army of 700 pro-slavery men

The Kansas-Nebraska Act of 1853.

attacked the free state stronghold of Lawrence, destroying the presses of two free soil newspapers, burning the hotel, and pillaging the town's stores.

The attack on Lawrence outraged John Brown, a fierce antislavery ideologue who had come with his family to Kansas to farm after a lifetime of drifting from occupation to occupation. On the night of May 24, Brown and a small band of followers murdered five pro-slavery settlers at Pottawatomie Creek in retaliation for slave-state attacks. The massacre set off further territorial violence in which Brown and his sons participated prominently.

THE ELECTION OF 1856
AND KANSAS AGAIN

In the election of 1856, James Buchanan narrowly beat John Charles Frémont, the first Republican presidential candidate, who ran on a platform demanding no slavery in the territories. The new president was an irresolute foppish, fussy, old bachelor of modest talents (we're trying to be generous here). Though a Pennsylvanian, he was a pro-Southern man who appointed many Southerners and "Northern men with Southern principles" to his cabinet. His tilt toward the South would offend many Northerners.

During the early months of Buchanan's term the situation in Kansas went from bad to worse. In February 1857 the pro-slavery territorial legislature called for a convention at Lecompton to write a state constitution and apply for admission to the Union. Pro-slavery territorial officials gerrymandered the delegate election districts for the convention to guarantee a pro-slavery majority, freesoilers boycotted the meeting, and the convention overwhelmingly passed a constitution that made Kansas a slave state.

What would Congress do now? Republicans, of course, denounced the state's constitution as fraudulent. And even Douglas said it was a denial of true "popular sovereignty"—the position that held that each territory should decide on its own whether to be slave or free. But the South and the Buchanan administration rushed to its support. In early 1858 sectional feelings ran so high that thirty members of Congress, in an early harbinger of the cooperative spirit that characterizes Republican-Democrat relations to this day, engaged in a wild fist fight on the House floor during an all-night debate over Kansas. In the end, the administration bulldozed, or shall we say steam-trained, the Senate into passing the Kansas statehood bill, but the House rejected it.

DRED SCOTT

Meanwhile, another source of political and sectional discord erupted. In March 1857 the Supreme Court, in the case of *Dred Scott v. Sanford,* decided that any law to exclude slavery from the territories, whether act of Congress or territorial legislature, was invalid, the position long taken by pro-slavery voters and politicians. Southerners crowed that they would finally have justice on the territorial issue.

The case involved a Missouri slave, Dred Scott, brought by his master to live in the Wisconsin Territory, free soil under the Missouri Compromise. He sued for his freedom on the grounds that living in a free territory made him free.

The case raised three important questions. First, did prolonged residence on free soil entitle Scott to his freedom? Second, was Scott, as a slave and a black, a citizen with the right to sue in the federal courts? Third, was the Missouri Compromise constitutional?

Dred Scott (1795–1858). According to the Supreme Court, he had "no rights which the white man was bound to respect."

The decision was a powerful blow against the position of both the "popular sovereignty" advocates and the freesoilers. The court decided that: (1) Dred Scott was still a slave; (2) as a slave and a black he was not a citizen, for blacks were—in one of the more memorable phrases in the history of American constitutional law—"beings of an inferior order . . . [and] had no rights which the white man was bound to respect"; and (3) his stay in Wisconsin territory did not free him because Congress could not constitutionally exclude slavery from a territory as it had tried to do under the Missouri Compromise. The victory for the Southern position was complete.

Republicans found themselves in a dilemma. The party's central plank, that Congress might exclude slavery from the territories, seemed now to have no legal basis.

THE LINCOLN-DOUGLAS DEBATES

The decision also seemed to nullify the "popular sovereignty" position, the notion that citizens could decide for themselves what the status of slaves in their state would be. The response came from Stephen Douglas during his campaign for reelection to the United States Senate in 1858. He proposed the Freeport Doctrine, so called because he enunciated it during a debate at

Abraham Lincoln (1809–1865), in a photograph taken in 1863.

Freeport, Illinois. Unless a territory passed slave codes to legalize and define slavery, no slave owner would bring his slaves to that region, Douglas observed. So the territories, even if they couldn't vote on whether to be slave or free, could by this logic in effect regulate slavery, no matter what the Supreme Court said. Douglas's Republican opponent was Abraham Lincoln, a lawyer from Springfield, Illinois, a former free soil Whig, newly converted to Republicanism.

THIS SHOW WILL NEVER WORK IN PRIME TIME, EVEN IF THEY PUT IT ON RIGHT AFTER 60 MINUTES

Both candidates toured Illinois speaking to large audiences of cheering partisans. They also met in seven face-to-face debates in towns scattered the length of the state. Lincoln—tall, weather-beaten, homely—looked like a gnarled tree trunk. He talked in a high tenor, and sawed the air with his hands. Douglas was a flamboyant orator with a booming voice and dramatic gestures, but his physical appearance was almost comical: squat and large-headed, a cartoon Humpty-Dumpty.

Douglas called the Republicans defenders of black equality and of policies that would destroy the Union. Lincoln denied any desire to encourage the social and political equality of black people. But he also declared "that this government was instituted to secure the blessings of freedom" and slavery was "an unqualified evil to the Negro, the white man, to the soil, and to the State."

JOHN BROWN'S BODY

*John Brown
(1800–1859).*

In mid-October 1859 John Brown and a small party of antislavery militants, with the goal of arming blacks and stirring up a slave insurrection, seized the federal arsenal at Harpers Ferry, Virginia. State and federal troops surrounded the arsenal and captured the would-be revolutionaries. Tried by a Virginia court for murder, treason, and insurrection, Brown was executed by hanging.

The South execrated the Brown raid. Nothing sent such a powerful pulse of fear through Southern hearts as the threat of "servile insurrection." Many Northerners, including Republicans, also deplored the Brown raid. But a minority in the North judged John Brown a saint and, after his execution, made him a martyr to freedom. Northern troops would go off to war in 1861 singing: "John Brown's body lies a-moldering in the grave, but his soul is marching on."

In the end Douglas was re-elected. But Lincoln had also won. Eastern Republicans became aware of an eloquent new voice in the West, and would remember it when the time came to select a candidate for president.

THE 1860 ELECTION

With sectional fears and resentments at a fever pitch in America, the Democratic national convention met at Charleston, South Carolina, in late April 1860. The party was bitterly divided on the issue of a federal slave code plank, which the Southerners demanded in order to bypass Douglas's Freeport formula. Douglas declared he would not run on such a platform.

When the northern position was sustained, fifty Southern delegates walked out. Meanwhile the remaining delegates were deadlocked. After 57 ballots the convention adjourned, to meet again in Baltimore, where Douglas was nominated, but not before the Southerners had bolted and nominated their own candidate, John C. Breckinridge, and adopted the federal slave code platform.

Meanwhile the Republicans had chosen Lincoln, a man of the West and a moderate on the slavery issue, as their candidate. The Republican platform attacked slavery, but also condemned John Brown.

The campaign that followed was the most momentous in American history. Neither the Douglas Democrats nor the Republicans had any chance in the slave states; the Republicans did not even bother getting on the ballot in the South. In Dixie the contest was primarily between Breckinridge and Tennessee's John Bell, an old Whig running on an evasive platform calling for nothing except national unity.

Historic decision no. 1

MAKING PLANS TO BE A SORE LOSER

The prospect that Lincoln would carry almost all the free states and win the election appalled Americans of several persuasions. In the North, Democrats and former Whigs foresaw disunion and the collapse of long-term economic ties with the South. Many working men considered the Republicans "nigger-lovers" whose policies would bring blacks north in droves to take white men's jobs. In the South, many feared that a Republican administration, even if unable constitutionally to touch slavery where established by state law, would appoint abolitionists to federal office, allow abolitionist literature to be disseminated in Dixie, and refuse to enforce the Fugitive Slave Law. In the end, Lincoln would unleash many John Browns to destroy Southern society. The only recourse, if Lincoln should win, was secession.

The result was a Republican electoral college victory. Lincoln's three opponents together won 2.8 million popular votes to his 1.9 million, but he carried all the free states and won a plurality in the electoral college. Lincoln would be president come March 1861.

STEPS TO SECESSION

Lincoln's election sent a twister of disgruntlement through the South. Seven states seceded before Lincoln was inaugurated, adopting a provisional constitution as the Confederate States of America with Jefferson Davis as president. Southern state officials then proceeded to seize federal property, including federal arsenals and forts. What should the government in Washington do? Should it try to get these facilities back? How? By negotiation? By force? How should federal laws be enforced and federal taxes collected?

ONE OF THE LAMEST OF LAME DUCKS

Buchanan, still president until March, dithered, afraid to use force to uphold federal authority, while moderate groups, in Congress and out, sought some formula that would be acceptable to both sides. But there was none.

Most Northerners were dismayed by the lower South's secession. It was unjustified and wrong-headed and a repudiation of the best government in the world they said. The Garrisonian abolitionists, however, welcomed the departure of the slave states, an act, they felt, that would finally free the nation of the evil taint of slavery. Horace Greeley, the *New York Tribune*'s antislavery editor advised letting "the erring sisters depart in peace."

THE SUMTER CRISIS

Lincoln's inaugural address held out an olive branch to the South, but also insisted that the Union was "perpetual." During the next few weeks, while Confederate commissioners negotiated in Washington for a peaceful severance from the Union, the two sides drifted onto a collision course over Fort Sumter, one of the few forts that federal authorities had not surrendered to the seceded states. South Carolina demanded that Sumter be evacuated and refused to allow supplies to be sent to Major Robert Anderson and his small force of eighty U.S. soldiers on the island. Lincoln decided to send a relief expedition.

SHOOTING WAR

Early on the morning of April 12, with the Union vessels already anchored off Charleston harbor, Confederate shore guns opened up on Major Anderson's men.

The Confederate batteries lobbed 4,000 rounds into the fort. Anderson fired back. After 34 hours, his ammunition low, Anderson surrendered. Not a single man on either side died but the nation's bloodiest and mostly costly war had begun.

SUMMARY

The bitter struggle over the territories—centering on which new states would be free and which slave—was the dominant theme of the decade before the Civil War.

The first Republican presidental candidate, John C. Frémont, ran unsuccessfully in 1856 against Democrat James Buchanan, and the campaign laid out the irreconcilable differences in world view that would soon lead to war.

When Lincoln was elected in 1860, the South realized its way of life was in jeopardy. Seven states had seceded before Lincoln took the oath of office.

CHAPTER 8

THE CIVIL WAR:
ONE NATION DIVISIBLE

YOU MUST REMEMBER THIS

Northern victory in the Civil War preserved the Union—Lincoln's primary goal—and ended slavery in the process. But if he could have preserved the Union without ending slavery, Lincoln would surely have done so.

IMPORTANT EVENTS

★ The First Battle at Bull Run, July 1861
★ Grant captures 14,000 Confederate soldiers at Fort Donelson, February, 1862
★ Farragut takes New Orleans, February 1862
★ Union victory at Antietam, September 1862
★ The Emancipation Proclamation, January 1863
★ Gettysburg, July 1863
★ Sherman marches into Georgia, May 1864
★ Lincoln reelected, November 1864
★ Confederate government evacuates Richmond, May 1865
★ Surrender at Appomattox, May 1865

"I'll take 'Civil War' for $800, Alex."

MOBILIZATION

O n April 15 Lincoln called 75,000 state militia into federal service for three months to put down the insurrection. By early June, North Carolina, Virginia, Tennessee, and Arkansas, outraged at the decision to use force, had joined the Confederacy.

WHO'S WHO

Do These Names Ring a Bell?

✵ **Abraham Lincoln** (1809-1865).
Sixteenth president of the United States. Lawyer, congressman, elected president in 1860 as a Republican.

✵ **Stephen Douglas** (1813-1861).
Congressman, secretary of state in 1840, justice

**WHO'S
HO**

(*continued*)

of Supreme Court in 1841, senator, unsuccessful candidate for president against Lincoln in 1860.

Robert E. Lee (1807-1870).
Top Confederate general of the Civil War.

George McClellan (1826-1885).
The Union general whom Lincoln replaced with Burnside in 1863. Ran for president in 1864, and was defeated by Lincoln. Became governor of New Jersey in 1878.

Pierre Beauregard (1818-1893).
West Point graduate who served in the Mexican War and was appointed a general in the Confederate Army in 1861. Failed to stop Sherman from moving through the South.

Jefferson Davis (1808-1889).
President of the Confederacy, 1861-65. Served in the Mexican War, then as senator from Mississippi. He was secretary of war from 1853 to 1857. Returned to Senate as leader of the States' Rights Party in 1860. Given amnesty in 1868 after spending two years in jail for treason.

William T. Sherman (1820-1891).
Union general, leader of famous March to the Sea through Georgia and the Carolinas.

THE LINEUPS

The tasks of organizing two nations to fight proved formidable. The Union was far more populous than the Confederacy—22 million to 9 million—and had three and a half times the number of men of military age. The North had the bulk of the nation's heavy industry, a superior railroad system, and control of the country's navy and most of is tiny regular army.

But the South had advantages as well. Many career officers of the regular army were Southerners and scores

BEHIND THE SCENES

Little-Known Players and Unsung Heroes

People, few of them white males, who don't always make it into the history books.

Frederick Douglass (1817-1895).
An escaped slave who became a leading abolitionist. An extraordinary public speaker, and the publisher of the abolitionist newspaper, *The North Star,* he was a tireless campaigner for full equality for blacks.

Harriet Tubman (1821-1913).
An ex-slave who raided plantations during the Civil War to free blacks, leading black and white troops, once liberating 750 slaves.

William Seward (1801-1872).
Lawyer, governor of New York, senator, and Lincoln's secretary of state, 1861-69. Negotiated purchase of Alaska from Russia in 1867. After that, Alaska was known as "Seward's Icebox."

of them resigned their commissions in early 1861 to take commands in the Confederate forces. The South was the more rural part of the nation and its young men were also more familiar than many Northerners with the shooting, riding, and outdoor living that were essential to soldiering. Finally, Dixie had strategic advantages. For the South to win it only had to survive; the North had to conquer. A war of conquest required superior numbers and material and as the would-be conquerors advanced they would move ever further from their supplies while their opponents would come ever closer to theirs.

One card Southerners expected to use was King Cotton. European nations were so dependent on cotton that to ensure their supply they would come to the Confederacy's rescue. To maximize the pressure on Britain and France, in early months of fighting Southerners imposed a virtual embargo on cotton. Almost none of the 1861 crop reached Europe.

INTERNAL DIVISIONS, NORTH AND SOUTH

Neither North nor South could claim the advantage of unity. Stephen Douglas and other War Democrats enthusiastically supported the Union cause, but other Democrats—called Copperheads by their opponents, after the poisonous snake—demanded that the South be allowed to leave the Union peacefully. At times, when he feared that Copperhead agitation threatened the Union war effort, Lincoln was not averse to suspending civil liberties. At one point, he banished former Democratic congressman, Clement Vallandigham, to the Confederacy for agitating against the Union draft.

The Republicans too were divided. The party had two wings. One, the Radicals, favored emancipation of the

"Lincolnesque, n'est-ce pas?*"*

slaves, the recruiting of black soldiers for the Union army, and harsh measures against "rebels," including confiscation of their property. The moderates resisted all these demands and often had the support of the cautious president. Still, however they tried, the Democrats in the North were unable to obstruct Republican policies, either war policies or other policies with long term goals.

In the Confederacy, support for the government was less than total. Unionist sentiment was strong in portions of the South where, as in the Appalachian region, there were few slaves and few plantations. In 1863-64 the western hill counties of Virginia broke away from the rest of the state to form West Virginia, a free state that fought for the Union. The Confederacy would also suffer from an excess of individual states' rights. The governors of Georgia and North Carolina frequently refused to cooperate with the Confederate authorities in Richmond. At one point, Governor Zebulon Vance of North Carolina declined to release uniforms in state warehouses to any but North Carolina troops while Robert E. Lee's troops were wearing rags.

MANPOWER PROBLEMS

Both sides faced manpower difficulties. All told 2.1 million men fought for the Union; 800,000 for the Confederacy. This was half the men of military age in the North and almost four-fifths the military-age white men in the South.

Lincoln soon asked Congress for power to recruit men for three years' service. Under these measures thousands of volunteers joined regiments organized by local leaders.

ALL DRESSED UP

Volunteers in the North, setting out with the enthusiasm and energy of young men who have never seen war, were determined to march on to Richmond and "hang Jeff Davis from a sour apple tree." Many of these took colorful names—"Yates Rangers," "Lincoln Guards," "New York Fire Zouaves"—and wore colorful uniforms. The Zouaves, for example, sported baggy red breeches, purple blouses, and red fezzes. It looked more like Mardi Gras in New Orleans than modern soldiers going off to war.

At first most volunteers were moved by patriotism or love of adventure, but almost from the beginning some communities met their quotas by offering bounties to enlistees. Later, bounties proved indispensable in raising a force.

The South relied at first on volunteers, but soon turned to bounties too. In 1862 the Confederate government adopted conscription. A year later, when the casualty lists began to grow, the Union government too was forced to pass a draft law—and draft riots in New York immediately followed. The draft was not entirely fair—there were many ways to get exemptions, including legally buying them, both in the North and the South. However unfair it seemed at the time, research shows that this was not a poor man's fight—both armies were a fairly good cross section of their populations, especially when allowance is made for the youth of the fighting men.

PAYING FOR THE WAR

The war cost a mint and strained the financial resources of both sides. The South, poorer and with more primitive financial institutions, found it difficult to raise taxes and quickly resorted to paper money. All told, by the end of the war, 1.5 billion Confederate dollars were in circulation. They quickly depreciated, driving prices up to almost a hundred times their 1860 level. The North too issued paper money—no government can resist the quick fix—but less of it ($500 million) in a much larger economy. These notes too depreciated but far less. Inflation in the North was kept under control not only by the smaller proportionate amount of paper money, but also because the Union government sold bonds too and laid heavy taxes on incomes and a wide array of commodities.

In Virginia City *(Warner, 1940), southern spies plot to steal a shipment of Yankee gold for the Confederacy.*

THE EARLY FIGHTING

Robert E. Lee
(1807–1870).
A man who
could lose
with dignity.

Neither side at first had an overall strategy beyond attack by the North and defense by the South. Unfortunately for the Union, attack was a very expensive stratagem. Both sides used highly accurate rifles, and although they were slow loading and slow firing, they proved devastating against advancing unprotected men. The disparities in losses would have been greater if the South, under General Robert E. Lee, had not itself adopted an aggressive defense that often took the form of costly sharp attacks against the advancing enemy.

BULL RUN: NO PICNICKING ALLOWED

The first major battle took place at Bull Run, twenty-five miles south of Washington where a Union army under General Irvin McDowell encountered a smaller force of Confederates under Pierre Beauregard on July 21. You remember the scene from every book you've read or movie you've seen about the Civil War—and it's all true: Ladies and gentlemen from Washington actually did go out to watch the battle as if it were going to be a picnic. A picnic, needless to say, it was not, and the Rebel forces inflicted a crushing defeat on the North. While the fighting seemed at first to go well for the Union troops, reinforcements under Joseph E. Johnston soon joined Beauregard. The fresh Southern soldiers, screaming the high-pitched "rebel yell," counterattacked, driving the tired Yankees back across the river. Retreat quickly turned to panic, and many of the Union men did not stop until they had arrived back in Washington exhausted, dispirited, and defeated. One Northern congressman was taken prisoner in the confused flight back to the capital.

Bull Run (also called First Manassas) in the end did the Union more good than harm. Southerners came to believe that one "Reb" could whip ten Yankees, while in fact the odds were much closer to even—and there were far more Yankees. At the same time, the defeat jolted the North into a realization of the enormous task ahead.

McDowell was demoted and the 34-year-old George B. McClellan made commander of the new Army of the Potomac. As new three-year volunteers flooded in McClellan drilled them rigorously and turned the raw recruits into disciplined soldiers. The nation hailed McClellan as a savior and the outpouring of adulation went to his head. He was soon treating the president with contempt and talking as if the fate of the whole country depended on him alone.

Unfortunately, the young general had even more serious faults than megalomania. He was a perfectionist who

Battle of Bull Run, or First Manassas.

kept demanding more men and equipment before advancing. Lincoln sat and watched, drumming his fingers like a man waiting for service in a bad restaurant, and finally asked sarcastically if he might borrow his army, since no one seemed to be using it.

LINCOLN AS COMMANDER-IN-CHIEF

Lincoln was one of the Union's outstanding human resources. Though not a military expert, he was a keen judge of character and eventually found the right combination of military talent to save the Union. He was also an adept politician. Pulled between conservatives who at times advised a negotiated peace and radicals who had other agendas besides suppressing the rebellion, he steered a middle course. The Union must come first and anything he did, including dealing with slavery, must be subordinate to saving the Union. Lincoln also added a powerful moral dimension to the Northern cause. His remarkable eloquence and grace under pressure lifted the spirits of the Northern people and ennobled the Northern endeavor. By contrast, Jefferson Davis, the Confederate president, able and well-meaning, was a fuss-budget who failed to inspire either his subordinates or the Southern people.

CAMPAIGNS EAST AND WEST

Watching McClellan during the eight months after Bull Run was like watching a baseball game during a four-hour rain delay. He dithered and delayed, collecting ever more men and supplies in the Washington area but refusing to move. Meanwhile, across the mountains in the West, Union troops under George Thomas and Ulysses Grant were defeating Confederate forces in Tennes-

President Abraham Lincoln and General McClellan, 1862.

see and Mississippi. On February 14, Grant captured Fort Donelson with 14,000 Confederate troops. At Shiloh he fended off a Confederate attack, both inflicting and sustaining heavy losses. In late April, the Union navy under Admiral David Farragut subdued the forts at New Orleans, allowing the Union army to take that strategic city, the largest in the Confederacy.

McCLELLAN BESTIRS HIMSELF

In early April the spirit finally moved McClellan and he advanced against Richmond, the Confederate capital,

ANTIETAM: WHERE MEN WERE MEN
AND IT TOOK AT LEAST FIVE BULLETS
TO MAKE THEM STOP WALKING

John B. Gordon was not a professional soldier, but he rose to the rank of lieutenant general in the Confederate army. Here's an excerpt from his account, published in 1904, of his experiences at Antietam. His account could almost serve as the thoughts of the Schwarzenegger robot in *Terminator*, had that movie been done in a voiced-over, stream-of-consciousness style:

"The first volley from the Union lines in my front sent a ball through the brain of the chivalric Colonel Tew, of North Carolina, to whom I was talking, and another ball through the calf of my right leg. [. . .] Higher up in the same leg I was again shot, but still no bone was broken. I was able to walk along the line and give encouragement to my resolute riflemen. . . . When later in the day the third ball pierced my left arm, tearing asunder the tendons and mangling the flesh, these devoted and big-hearted men . . . pleaded with me to leave them and go to the rear. . . . A fourth ball ripped through my shoulder, leaving its base and a wad of clothing in its track. I could still stand and walk . . . I looked at the sun. It moved very slowly. . . . I had gone but a short distance when I was shot down by a fifth ball, which struck me squarely in the face, and passed out barely missing the jugular vein. I fell forward and lay unconscious with my face in my cap; it would seem that I might have been smothered by the blood running into my cap from this last wound but for the act of some Yankee, who, as if to save my life, had at a previous hour during the battle, shot a hole through the cap, which let the blood out."

from the east. But he vastly overrated Confederate strength. When he finally engaged the Confederates, led by Lee, the battles were inconclusive. The Confederates lost more men than the Union, but McClellan retreated anyway. In late July Lincoln ordered the Army of the Potomac back to Washington.

Still, Lincoln kept McClellan in command, even after his failure to help John Pope at the Second Battle of Bull Run (August 29-30) produced another serious Union defeat. Then, in mid-September, McClellan met Lee's advance northward into Maryland at the Battle of Antietam, one of the bloodiest of the war. Owing to the Union general's failure to use his reserves, the battle was a draw on the field, and Lee escaped. But since he retreated south, McClellan had at long last achieved at least a technical victory.

SLAVERY AND THE WAR

Antietam was more important for its political than for its military consequences. From the outset antislavery leaders had seen the war as an opportunity to destroy slavery and had urged Lincoln to make emancipation one of the Union's war aims. Lincoln, for fear of driving the border slave states into the arms of the Confederacy and obscuring the goal of preserving the Union, postponed action on slavery for many months. In a response to Horace Greeley's editorial demanding emancipation, he declared: "If I could save the Union without freeing any slave, I would do it; and if I could save it by freeing all the slaves I would do it; and if I could save it by freeing some and leaving others alone, I would also do that."

By mid-1862, however, he had concluded that slavery was a powerful bulwark of the Confederate cause.

Though slaves did not fight for the South, they worked its fields and factories and released white men for the Confederate army and navy. Blacks, moreover, were a potential pool of military manpower for the North. Promise them freedom and thousands of Southern blacks would flee and join the Union army. Blacks in contact with Union troops were already deserting and, under the heading of "contraband of war," were being put to use by Union generals as laborers.

Now, in the wake of Antietam, a qualified Union victory, Lincoln issued the Preliminary Emancipation Proclamation under his war powers as commander-in-chief. On January 1, 1863, it stated, in all areas still in rebellion, all slaves would be then, thenceforward, and forever free. It justified emancipation solely on military grounds, suggested a program of voluntary departure of free blacks for other countries, and asked the loyal slave states to gradually free their slaves by state action. When, on January 1, the final proclamation was declared in effect, most slaves were still under Confederate control and were unaffected by the document.

WHOM DID THE EMANCIPATION PROCLAMATION EMANCIPATE?

Almost nobody. It didn't apply to slaves in the border states whose loyalty Lincoln so much wanted to preserve. And it didn't affect slaves in the parts of Southern states already under Union control. The states that it did affect—those "in rebellion"—of course ignored it. Insofar as any slaves were freed there during the war, they freed themselves as Union troops advanced. But the political point was made, and the true end of slavery was accomplished with the passage of the thirteenth amendment on December 18, 1865.

Yet the proclamation marked the effective end of the evil institution. Even in the lower South, beyond Union control, slavery began to crumble. Aware of the Union's goals, blacks fled the plantation for the Yankee lines at the merest hint of Union troops approaching. In effect blacks liberated themselves. By the time Congress passed the Thirteenth Amendment to the Constitution declaring slavery illegal in all the United States, the institution had collapsed virtually everywhere.

BLACK SOLDIERS

Blacks earned the gratitude of Unionists by their bravery and skill as soldiers. The first black regiments had been organized in early 1863. Officered overwhelmingly by whites and paid less than white soldiers, the black recruits nonetheless fought well. At first the Confederate authorities threatened to shoot captured members of black regiments, whether officers or privates, but relented when Lincoln threatened retaliation. In all, almost 200,000 black men served in the Union army and navy. Their brave record helped reduce, though not eliminate, race prejudice among Northern white people.

THE HOME FRONTS

What happened on the home front, especially in the North, was in many ways more important than what happened on the battlefields. Economic historians now believe that the war interfered with real economic growth by reducing the civilian labor force and deflecting capital into non-productive channels. Soldiers, cannon, and gunboats are simply not as productive as artisans, plows, and iron furnaces. Yet after the early months, the North wore an air of prosperity. Manufacturers, government contractors, and farmers made money supplying the government and they—and their wives—spent it conspiciously. While men were dying in agony at Gettysburg, the luxury stores in Philadelphia and New York were thronged with shoppers, just as in post-Gulf War Baghdad, luxury items are still available to embargo-busting profiteers.

NO GRIDLOCK IN WASHINGTON

If the war shows up as a downward blip on the total output charts, it set the stage for the economic take-off of the last third of the century. With the South out of the Union and the Democrats reduced to a rump, the old Hamilton-Clay economic nationalism triumphed. The thiry-seventh Congress, with overwhelming Republican majorities, enacted a Homestead Act granting a free farm in the West to almost anyone who applied, established agricultural and technical colleges in each state supported by land grants (the Morrill Land Grant College Act), passed the Pacific Railroad Act for a central-route railway to the Pacific Coast subsidized by federal bonds and federal lands (so much for the myth of the lone cowboy conquering the west), raised the tariff to shield American industry against foreign competition, and adopted a National Banking Act that created a system of federally chartered commercial banks. One historian, with some exaggeration, has described the legislative program of the thirty-seventh Congress as a blueprint for modern America.

SOUTHERN DEPRIVATIONS

It was hard to find positive effects of the war on the

Southern home front. Output fell, hyper-inflation raged, food was in short supply, the Union blockade was irritating to the rich and devastating for the poor. Even southern farmers who raised their own food suffered. With the young men "gone for a soldier," the old, the female, the black tried to take up the slack but seldom succeeded. There was often less food to go around, particularly since salt was in short supply making it difficult to preserve meat and vegetables. In Richmond, in 1863, hungry women broke into shops and warehouses shouting "Bread, bread!" and President Davis and a hastily gathered company of militia had to rush to the scene and threaten to fire on the crowd before the insurrection was ended.

Southern fears of a slave uprising, with so many white men in the army, proved to be misplaced. By and large, the Confederacy's 3 million slaves continued to labor peaceably in Dixie's fields and homes. And their submission is easily explained. Even if they yearned for freedom, they still remained a minority among a heavily armed majority. And besides, the Union meant little to them.

The Emancipation Proclamation and the advance of Union troops deep into the South changed all that. Though white Southerners were cosmically uninterested in spreading the news of Lincoln's proclamation, it seeped through to the farms and plantations and often riveted the attention of the black inhabitants. Yet they usually waited until Union forces approached and then pulled up stakes—and as much else of master's chattels as they could—and fled to the advancing Yankees. Sherman's troops were accompanied by ragged groups of self-liberated slaves often riding their owners' wagons and mules to keep up with the blue-clad Union soldiers.

DIPLOMACY

Cotton diplomacy failed. The South withheld cotton from Britain, but Britain had plenty of cotton, so no one much cared. Still, there were some hard moments for the Union. In late 1861 the Union navy intercepted a British merchant ship, the *Trent,* and removed two Confederate commissioners on the way to Europe. The British were not amused, but Lincoln quickly concluded that one war at a time was enough, apologized, and authorized release of the two men. Tempers soon cooled.

Thereafter, the principle strain on British-American relations was the U.S. naval blockade of southern ports and Confederate counter measures. The Union inherited most of the prewar American navy and then expanded it rapidly. The Union military used navy river gun boats effectively in joint operations on southern rivers. But most of the fleet was assigned to blockade duty along the Atlantic and Gulf coasts to prevent the South from exporting its goods abroad and from receiving back badly needed supplies for the military and for civilians. Despite swift blockade runners and smuggling from the West Indies and Mexico, the Union blockade became ever more effective.

To meet the Union naval challenge the Confederacy relied on British shipyards. A direct threat to the blockade were the Laird rams, two ironclads ordered by Confederate agents from a Scottish firm and capable of sinking any of the wooden blockade vessels of the Union fleet by the simple expedient of ramming into them. Fortunately, the American ambassador induced the British government to seize the vessels before they were completed.

Though secretary of state William Seward and American ambassador in London Charles Francis Adams managed to prevent a rupture, by late 1862 the British and French were prepared to recognize the Confederacy and force the Union to accept foreign mediation. Such a move would undoubtedly have established Southern independence. But after Antietam, the British decided that the Confederacy was still far from achieving its independence. They canceled plans to consider recognition and rejected a French proposal for forced mediation. In the end, the Confederacy could not count on Europe to rescue it from defeat.

CONFEDERATE DEFEAT

Meanwhile the fighting and the dying went on.

In November 1862 Grant succeeded McClellan, and took Vicksburg and the last Confederate bases on the Mississippi in the spring and summer. By early July, he had cut the Confederacy in two at the Mississippi. In March 1864 Lincoln gave Grant overall command of the Union armies.

During the summer of 1863, Union armies were also successful in the East when Lee invaded Pennsylvania hoping to shock the North into peace negotiations. The North was not shocked, and General George Meade marched to Gettysburg, where his victory over Robert E. Lee marked the turning point of the war.

Unionists' joy at the Gettysburg victory was marred by the draft riots in New York when thousands of the city's working people, angry at the beginnings of conscription, attacked Republican newspapers and black people. For four days, the mobs rampaged out of control until troops from Meade's army were rushed to the city to stop the mayhem.

BLOODY GETTYSBURG

The Gettysburg battlefield favored the defense. Flat fields alternated with hills, naked rock formations, and ridges. The Union forces were entrenched atop the ominously named Cemetery Ridge with most of the Confederates on the plain below to the west.

After two days of bloody skirmishing Lee decided on a frontal assault against Meade's center. About one o'clock on July 3 the Confederates opened the attack with a furious cannonade that exceeded anything ever seen before on an American battlefield. The barrage failed to still the Union batteries and when George Pickett's division of 14,000 men charged across the open field at three o'clock they ran into a wall of shell and shot. When they approached the entrenched Yanks, Ohio, Vermont, and New York regiments swung out from behind their walls and raked the Confederates with rifle fire from both flanks. After an hour the attackers reeled back to their own lines.

Gettysburg was a slaughterhouse. Of the 14,000 men who made up Pickett's Charge, only half survived. As Lee rode among his exhausted troops he moaned: "It is all my fault. It is I who have lost this fight. . . ."

AFTER GETTYSBURG

Despite the success at Gettysburg, there were many dark days for the Union ahead. In the spring of 1864 Grant launched a major campaign to capture Richmond from the North. In a series of inconclusive battles (the Wilderness, Spotsylvania, Cold Harbor, Petersburg) he painfully inched forward, finally settling down to an extended siege. Union losses were heavy and the public began to talk of "butcher Grant." But Confederate casualties were also high, and the North could afford the drain far more easily than the South.

In May 1864 William T. Sherman with 100,000 blue-clad men set out from their base at Chattanooga and swung into Georgia. Sherman intended to carry the war deep into the enemy's heartland even if it meant exposing his long lines of supply. In early September he captured Atlanta.

For the Lincoln administration it was not a moment too soon. Though retired from the army, McClellan had not left public life. In August 1864 he won the Democratic nomination for president on a platform that called for an immediate end to hostilities. The costly stalemate in Virginia fed Northern gloom during the summer of 1864 and many believed that the ticket of Lincoln and Andrew Johnson might well suffer defeat. But Sherman's victory at Atlanta turned the tide. In November the Lincoln-Johnson ticket won by 400,000 votes.

Sherman, determined to hear the South scream for mercy but offering none, took Savannah on the coast in late December and then turned through the Carolinas carrying out his scorched earth policies all the way. Ordered to "forage liberally on the country," for supplies Sherman's "bummers" looted and burned private homes wholesale. On February 17 his army entered Columbia, the capital of South Carolina. Shortly after, a devastating fire swept the city, a conflagration that few Southerners doubted had been deliberately set.

As Sherman moved northward, Grant finally broke the stalemate in northern Virginia and pushed on toward Richmond. The Confederate government, deprived of supplies, money, and manpower, tried desperately to shore up the sinking cause by authorizing slave enlistment in the Confederate army. It came too late. On April 2 the Davis government evacuated Richmond after destroying bridges, factories, arsenals, and government property. Soon after, Union troops occupied the Confederate capital. On April 5 Lincoln visited the still smoking city under escort of a black cavalry troop.

Lee's army, much reduced but still intact, sought to escape the Yankees but was quickly trapped. On April 9 Lee and Grant met at Appomattox Courthouse and worked out terms of surrender. Lee's men would be allowed to return home with their private property after surrendering all military equipment. In the west, fighting dragged on for a few weeks longer, but to all intents and purposes the war was over.

John Wilkes Booth (1838–1865). An actor's publicity shot.

On the evening of April 14, Lincoln and a party of friends attended a play at Ford's Theater in Washington. In the middle of the performance a shot rang out and John Wilkes Booth, an actor and Confederate patriot, leapt to the stage shouting Virginia's motto "Thus Always to Tyrants." The president died early the next morning. Booth was at large for two weeks, but was cornered in a burning barn and shot to death by Union troops. Several suspected accomplices were captured, and four were hanged. The war had ended in Union tragedy after all.

The war had been a catastrophe. Over 350,000 Union soldiers had died; some 258,000 Confederate. These losses, plus the many wounded, represent between 33% and 40% of the combined Union and Confederate forces, the highest casualty rates of any American war. Add to this the economic costs and the profound disruption of ordinary life and one can only conclude that the war was the worst human disaster that ever befell the United States. Yet it had ended slavery, and surely that was more than a trivial subtraction from the sum of human misery.

SUMMARY

⏱ Hostilities began with Lincoln's decision to use force to uphold federal authority in preventing states from seizing federal property.

⏱ Lincoln as commander-in-chief was perhaps the North's greatest human resource. He was a keen judge of character, eloquent, graceful under pressure, always steering a middle course between conservatives and radicals.

⏱ The Emancipation Proclamation of 1863, while having little immediate impact on slavery, was nevertheless the beginning of the end of the peculiar institution.

⏱ The Confederacy, smaller than the Union, poorer, less industrialized, failed to find either allies abroad or resources at home to create an independent nation.

⏱ The Civil War ended slavery and a Southern way of life, but Lincoln's primary goal was always the preservation of the Union.

CHAPTER 9

RECONSTRUCTION
REUNITING A NATION

YOU MUST REMEMBER THIS

Reconstruction created a solid Democratic South, a disenfranchised black peasantry, and a section of the country that would increasingly lose touch with the forces of "progress."

IMPORTANT EVENTS

- ★ Andrew Johnson becomes president, 1865
- ★ Fourteenth Amendment, 1866
- ★ Reconstruction Act, 1867
- ★ Johnson impeached, 1867
- ★ Grant elected president, 1868
- ★ Fifteenth Amendment, 1870
- ★ The Ku Klux Klan Acts, 1870-71
- ★ Hayes elected, 1876

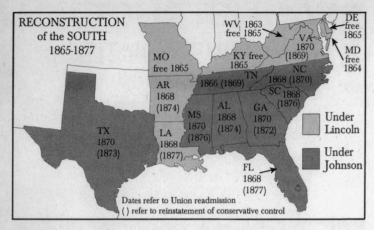

This map depicts states as they were governed during the Reconstruction.

THE GREAT WAR OF BROTHERS WAS OVER. NOW WHAT?

Lots of problems remained. First there was resentment. Northerners would not easily forget the 350,000 Union dead, the brutal Southern prisoner-of-war camps, the assassination of Lincoln, the billions of dollars expended to put down the wicked rebellion. Southerners—white Southerners, that is—would remember the 260,000 dead "Johnny Rebs," the scorched-earth policy of Sherman's bummers in Georgia and South Carolina, and the total destructon of Dixie's labor system. For years afterwards Northern veterans would heed Republican politicians' exhortation to remember Southern misdeeds and "vote as you shot," a go-for-the-jugular slogan that makes today's implicit race baiting (e.g. the Willie Horton TV ads used against Governor Dukakis in 1988) look tame. The white South, for its part, would

WHO'S WHO ☞

Do These Names Ring a Bell?

※ Andrew Johnson (1808-1875).
Seventeenth president of the United States, the only president ever to be impeached. Congressman, governor of Tennessee, became president on Lincoln's death in 1865.

※ Ulysses S. Grant (1822-1885).
Union general, eighteenth president of the United States, 1868-76.

※ Rutherford B. Hayes (1822-1893).
Congressman, governor of Ohio, elected nineteenth president of the United States in 1876.

※ Thaddeus Stevens (1792-1868).
Member of Congress, Republican leader, and chairman of the trial of Andrew Johnson, 1868.

※ Horace Greeley (1811-1872).
Newspaper editor and publisher, antislavery editorialist, and unsuccessful candidate for president in 1872.

retreat into the legend of the Lost Cause, a noble, if doomed, strike for freedom crushed by the sheer numbers and might of a crude Yankee business civilization.

ANDREW JOHNSON ASSUMES THE HELM

Presiding over the early phases of Reconstruction, the effort to reunite the nation after four years of civil war,

*Andrew Johnson
(1808–1875).*

was president Andrew Johnson, a man catapulted into office by the tragic events at Ford's Theater just days after Lee's surrender. Johnson was a Southerner, but a man from the East Tennessee hills where there were few slaves and no plantations, and the people there liked it that way. They also liked the Union, and refused to go along with the rest of the state when it joined the Confederacy in 1861. A fierce Unionist, Johnson was the only U.S. Senator from a Confederate state who remained in Congress after secession, and he was rewarded by the Republicans by being put on the ballot with Lincoln in 1864. He took the oath of office while Lincoln's body was being prepared for burial.

Johnson started out in life as an illiterate tailor, whose wife eventually taught him to read. He was always touchy about his origins and, however open he was to their flattery and manipulation, he hated the high and mighty planter class. He also had the prejudices of poor whites against blacks. Maybe they were now free, he felt, but that certainly didn't mean that these lesser beings were going to assume civic equality with whites.

Johnson's anti-planter, anti-Confederate resentments showed in his first stab at Reconstruction. He granted amnesty to Confederate soldiers who took an oath of allegiance (except those who owned property worth $20,000 or more), and appointed provisional governors for seven Southern states, empowering them to call conventions of loyal citizens to change the Southern state constitutions so that they accepted the end of slavery, repealed their secession ordinances, and repudiated Southern state war debts. He attached no other strings. Nothing need be said about giving former slaves the vote, or expressing regret for the awful war.

ANDREW JOHNSON
. . . .

In real life, outside of fiction, it's tough to find examples of true tragedy in the careers of politicians. But Andrew Johnson comes close. He sided with the Union against his own Democratic party in Tennessee when it came to secession, and for his staunch and principled Unionism, was rewarded by the Republicans with the vicepresidency. When he tried to treat the Confederacy with leniency after the war, his Republican allies turned on him. He was impeached with little except partisan political motives, since he'd done nothing impeachable, and he was nearly convicted. He was unpolished in manner, often tactless in speech (he once implied in a public address that the Radical Republicans had had something to do with the assassination of Lincoln—well before such conspiracy theories became fashionable, unfortunately), but he was kind and sympathetic in personality, with a shyness some mistook for coldness. In the end, he was accused of violating the same Constitution which he had tried so hard to uphold, his policies were rejected by the people he felt he had served in good conscience, and he left the presidency beaten and bitter.

The new governments reconstituted under the Johnson plan thumbed their noses at Northern sensibilities. As they waited for Congress to admit their newly elected House and Senate delegations, they passed Black Codes—hateful laws preventing blacks from voting, serving on juries, or sharing public accommodations. Under various vagrancy laws, blacks without jobs could be forcibly apprenticed to employers to work under duress. It seemed to many Northerners that this was little more than an attempt to restore slavery in spite of it all. So harsh was the Mississippi code that the editor of the *Chicago Tribune* warned "the men of the North will con-

LIVING FREE IN LOUISIANA

Ordinances in St. Landry Parish Louisiana established in July 1865 and approved and enforced by Union army officials included, among other rules, the following:

1. "No negro shall be allowed to pass within the limits of said parish without special permit in writing from his employer."
2. "Every negro who shall be found absent from the residence of his employer after ten o'clock at night . . . shall pay a fine of five dollars. . . ."
3. "No negro shall be permitted to keep or rent a house within said parish."
4. "Every negro is required to be in the service of some white person or former owner. . . ."
5. "No public meetings or congregations of negroes shall be allowed within said parish after sunset. . . ."
6. "No negro shall be permitted to preach, exhort, or otherwise declaim to congregations of colored people, without a special permission in writing. . . ."
7. "No negro shall sell, barter, or exchange any articles of merchandise . . . without the special written permission of his employer. . . ."

Any violations of these rules was punishable by ". . . confining the body of the offender within a barrel placed over his or her shoulders, in the manner practiced in the army, such confinement not to continue longer than 12 hours. . . ."

vert the state of Mississippi into a frog pond before they will allow such laws to disgrace one foot of soil in which the bones of our soldiers sleep and over which the flag of freedom waves."

CONGRESS TAKES CHARGE

Johnson's fiercest opponents were the Radical Republicans who dominated Congress. Despite their name, which may suggest some kind of socialism or anti-capitalist ideology, these men supported protective tariffs, a sound currency, government subsidies to build railroads, and federal appropriations to improve rivers and harbors, all measures that business leaders favored. If they were radical in any way it was in their view that the South must change its racial attitudes. Johnson and the Radicals were at each other's throats in part because the president disliked their big-government, pro-business philosophy.

FORTY ACRES AND A MULE

Thaddeus Stevens (1792–1868). "Forty Acres and a Mule."

The head Radical in the House was Thaddeus Stevens of Pennsylvania, an iron manufacturer whose hatred of former Confederates, people said, came from the destruction of his iron mill by Lee's troops in their 1863 invasion of Pennsylvania. Stevens clearly did not enjoy seeing his property torched, but in fact, his animus toward the white South derived from his deep commitment to racial equality. A grim-faced man who wore an ill-fitting, jet-black wig, he wanted to guarantee full citizenship to the "freedmen" in the South. By all means assure them the vote. But go beyond this. The government should confiscate the great Southern estates and confer forty acres of land on each black family. This would compensate blacks for their years of bondage and at the same time "humble the proud traitors."

It is not surprising that blacks themselves were invariably Radicals. The educated Northern black leadership demanded the vote as black men's due. Frederick Doug-

Frederick Douglass (1817–1895). The Dean of Black Radicals.

lass, the craggy, white-haired dean of black Radicals, headed a delegation to the White House in 1866 to demand that Johnson require suffrage as a condition of Reconstruction. The president parried their arguments and when they left exclaimed that Douglass was "just like any nigger . . ."—he "would sooner cut a white man's throat than not." In the South the former slaves craved even more; like Stevens, they wanted "land for the landless." And many believed that they would get it. In the months after Appomattox rumors circulated that the government was going to distribute "forty acres and a mule" (hence the name of filmmaker Spike Lee's production company) to all black families to enable them to support themselves as independent farmers.

The Radicals had many enemies besides Johnson. Even in the North many voters sided with the president. Most Democrats hated the Radicals. These extremists, they charged, were "vindictive" toward the South and, worse, were pro-black. When, soon after the war, several Northern states voted to end disfranchisement of black residents, Democrats voted overwhelmingly against the change, and not enough Republicans supported granting black males the vote to overcome the deeply embedded Northern racism that had survived the end of slavery. As for the schemes to create a new class of small black farmers, in the end even the Radicals were not radical enough. It was sufficient, many said, to give blacks the vote. As full citizens they could protect themselves against white Southern conservatives and eventually acquire property on their own.

But Congress had been in recess when Lincoln was

shot, so Johnson could do as he pleased. When it convened in December 1865, it attacked what Johnson had
done. Look what his leniency toward the former rebels
had accomplished: the Black Codes, race riots in New
Orleans and Memphis, and an outrageous roster for the
Southern delegations applying for admission to Congress:
nine former Confederate congressmen, four Confederate
generals, and the Confederate vice-president, Alexander
Stephens! An outrage! Congress sent them home and established a Joint Committee on Reconstruction to manage
the process of restoring the South to the Union.

The president and the Republican Congressional leadership were two giant ships on a collision course. In the
months that followed, they would crash into one another, scattering bodies and debris in every direction.

The first noisy clash came over the president's veto in
early 1866 of a bill empowering the Freedmen's Bureau
to prosecute persons who violated the rights of the ex-
slaves. The bureau, a wartime agency organized to aid
refugees and administer abandoned Southern lands, had
helped former slaves and was a favorite target of conservatives. Eventually Congress passed the bill over Johnson's veto. The president also vetoed the Civil Rights Act
which gave blacks citizenship as well as other civil rights
that the Southern states had refused to grant. Congress
overrode the veto again.

On June 16, after extensive hearings and investiga-
tions, the Joint Committee on Reconstruction proposed
an amendment to the Constitution to place the rights of
persons as against the states beyond any possible constitutional challenge. The Fourteenth Amendment declared black Americans to be citizens and forbade states
to "deprive any person of life, liberty, or property without due process of law" or "deny to any person . . . the
equal protection of the laws." In addition it sought to
confer the vote on most Southern blacks by requiring

VOTING RIGHTS, 1865-1870

Giving former slaves full citizenship isn't as easy as it sounds. In fact, it took the Emancipation Proclamation plus no fewer than three amendments to the Constitution before it was fully accomplished. In 1865, the Thirteenth Amendment said quite simply that "neither slavery nor involuntary servitude . . . shall exist within the United States." The Fourteenth Amendment (1868) added that "All persons born or naturalized in the United States . . . are citizens of the United States and of the state wherein they reside," and it asserted that if states didn't start counting black people as citizens, their representation in Congress would be reduced. But it took the Fifteenth Amendment, ratified in 1870, to finally assure that "the right of citizens of the United States to vote shall not be denied or abridged by the United States or by any state on account of race, color, or previous condition of servitude."

that any state that deprived adult males of the vote would have its representation in Congress reduced proportionately. (In the Fifteenth Amendment, passed in 1870, this roundabout method of enfranchising blacks was replaced by a straight prohibition of voting restrictions based on race.)

JOHNSON SPEAKS FOR HIMSELF (AND LIVES TO WISH HE HADN'T)

By mid-1866 relations between the president and the Radical congress had reached the breaking point. That summer and fall, now totally alienated from the Republicans, Johnson sought to create a coalition of conservatives from both parties to oppose the Radicals. In late August the president went out campaigning against the

Radicals in the Congressional elections. He lost his cool when hecklers challenged him. "Why not hang Thad Stevens?" he shouted at one rally. At another he tearfully compared himself to Jesus (Jim and Tammy Faye Baker, move over). He too favored forgiveness and was being martyred for his views. The president's efforts backfired. The Republicans won an astounding victory and retained a three-to-one majority in both houses of Congress.

Back in session, Congress passed a Reconstruction Act that swept away all Johnson's work. The 1867 law divided the Southern states into five military districts under the

JOHNSON-GATE, OR HOW CONGRESS LEARNED TO STOP WORRYING AND HATE ANDREW JOHNSON

What, exactly, did Johnson do to get himself in such trouble?

He violated something called the Tenure of Office Act. This act was passed by the Republican congress in March, 1867 specifically to deprive Johnson of a part of his power. The act provided that the president could not dismiss any officer appointed by and with the consent of the Senate. The act was intended to provoke: It meant that the president could not fire his own cabinet officers, which no president could tolerate. Edwin Stanton, the secretary of war, was a friend of the Radicals, so Johnson fired him—both because he couldn't stand him, and because it would be a good way to test the constitutionality of the Tenure of Office Act before the Supreme Court. But he never got as far as the Supreme Court—before he could, the Senate impeached him, exactly as they had planned to do, using this as an excuse. The case against Johnson was extremely weak, but the partisan Senate came within one vote of canning him: 35-19 in favor.

control of Union generals. Only after each state had called a constitutional convention elected by universal male suffrage, adopted a constitution that authorized blacks to vote, and ratified the Fourteenth Amendment, (extending due process to blacks) would their representatives and senators be readmitted into Congress. Johnson vetoed the Reconstruction Act of 1867; Congress—you're getting the picture by now—overrode him still again.

IMPEACHMENT: HE VETOED US, NOW WE'LL VETO HIM

Johnson was hobbled by the efforts of the Radicals, but not crippled—he could still interpret the Reconstruction laws to favor his views and he could still use his pardoning power to restore white conservatives to their lands and their political rights. The real hotheads were convinced that for Radical Reconstruction to work Johnson had to be removed from office. The only way was by impeachment, a drastic step that had seldom

BEN WADE: JOHNSON'S IMPEACHMENT INSURANCE?

The president *pro tempore* (that's Latin for "temporary") presides over the Senate when the vice-president is absent, his power stemming more from the fact that he is usually the senior senator from his party than from any powers of the office itself. If Johnson had been impeached, there was no vice-president to replace him, and the president *pro tem* of the Senate, then as now, was next in line. This was Ohio's Ben Wade, one of the Radicals' own. That enough Republicans disliked Wade, however, may have been one of the things that saved Johnson's neck.

been used against any federal official, and never against a president. An impeachment drive in early 1867 failed after moderate Republicans chickened out, but in mid-1867 the president handed the Radicals the weapons they needed against him by attempting to remove Secretary of War Stanton, a Radical in the enemy camp, and several pro-Racial generals in the South. The Stanton removal seemed to violate the Tenure of Office Act and provided grounds for Radical claims of malfeasance in office. On February 24, 1868 the House of Representatives voted to impeach Johnson and drew up charges to be presented to the Senate, the body which would try him.

The Senate refused to convict—just barely—but it didn't matter. Johnson, chastened, thereafter stayed out of the Reconstruction process. One by one, under the Radical program, the Southern states were re-admitted to the Union.

THE GENERAL BECOMES PRESIDENT

In the presidential election of 1868 the Democrats nominated Horatio Seymour of New York on a platform that called the Reconstruction acts "a flagrant usurpation of power ... unconstitutional, revolutionary, and void." The Republicans turned to the grizzled, laconic war hero, Grant, who appealed to a growing public weariness with his call "Let us have peace." In the end, Grant won, carrying most of the former Confederacy, and all but three Northern states. Now the executive branch too would be Radical.

SOUTHERN LIVING

Meanwhile the South was on a social and economic roller coaster. Former slaves had tested their new status soon after the fighting ceased by leaving the plantations, visiting friends and family in other communities, and going to the towns for a little urban excitement. Whites, Northern and Southern alike, worried that the ex-slaves would not work and the South would never recover from the war's devastation. Freedmen's Bureau agents tried to draw up employment contracts between ex-slaves and white planters, but these proved hard to enforce, especially with cash so scarce in the immediate postwar South. Blacks, of course, would have preferred "forty acres and a mule," but these were not forthcoming. A few lucky freedmen were able to save some money and buy land; another small group were able to take up land in the Plains under the 1862 Homestead Act. But most of the ex-slaves had to settle for share-crop tenant farming, especially in the cotton belt.

This system was at best half a loaf. In exchange for their labor black cotton farmers would rent land and a house from a white landlord. When the crop was sold the farmer would pay the landlord half the crop as rent. Not only did blacks use this arrangement; a substantial number of poor white farmers did so as well.

The system had both an upside and a downside. Unlike slavery or gang labor under a foreman, it provided some personal autonomy. Black families had their own home and their own piece of land to farm. For the first time some black women had an opportunity to leave the fields and be home-makers; black children could go to school; black farmers could set their own work pace. All in all, under the sharecrop system, blacks improved their income over slavery days by a large amount.

Yet the new system did not bring heaven-on-earth. Share croppers remained among the poorest Americans. They had no incentive to improve the land or adopt new farming methods. Coupled with the falling price of cotton, this circumstance led to small returns for their

BEHIND THE SCENES

Little-Known Players and Unsung Heroes

People, few of them white males, who don't always make it into the history books.

Frances Ellen Watkins Harper (1825-1911).
Abolitionist lecturer, spoke all over the South after the war. She was a founder of the National Association of Colored Women. She wrote the first published novel by a black woman.

Sojourner Truth (1777-1883).
An ex-slave, a campaigner for women's rights, and a recruiter of black troops during the Civil War.

Henry McNeal Turner (1834-1915).
Escaped from a Georgia plantation at the age of 15, taught himself to read and write, read lawbooks while he worked in a law office in Baltimore, and medical books while he worked as a handyman in a medical school there, was chaplain in a Negro regiment during the Civil War, and was elected to the first post-war legislature in Georgia.

Victoria Woodhull (1838-1927).
In 1868 Woodhull and her sister became the first female New York stockbrokers. In 1871 she became the first woman to appear before Congress, when she testified vigorously in favor of women's rights. In 1872 she ran for president on the Equal Rights Party ticket.

BEHIND THE SCENES

(*continued*)

Myra Bradwell (1831-1894).
In 1868, she founded and edited the *Chicago Legal News*. Bradwell qualified for admission to the Illinois bar, but admission was denied because of her sex. Campaigned successfully for an Illinois law that, in 1882, banned exclusion from any profession on the basis of sex.

Susan B. Anthony (1820-1906).
Schoolteacher by profession, fearless crusader for women's rights by conviction, Anthony was a leader in the suffrage, temperance and abolition movements. She was arrested and indicted for attempting to vote in the 1872 Presidential election.

labor. At the same time many share croppers were linked to an expensive and entangling credit system. Typically they bought on credit at a local general store goods like cloth, flour, hardware, pork, and small treats. The merchant, to insure payment, got a lien (a kind of mortgage) on the farmer's crop. When the crop was sold, the farmer paid the debt—if he could. But since credit goods were expensive and cotton prices were usually weak he often fell short. Thousands of share croppers became permanently indebted to merchants, near-peons, forced to do business only with their creditors.

At the same time, the system fastened cotton culture like a noose around the South's neck. Merchants encouraged only the growing of cotton, the cash crop they knew, and when the price fell, the South produced more and more of the white bolls. This response forced cotton prices still lower, ensuring that the South would fall further behind the nation in every measure of wealth and comfort.

SOUTHERN POLITICS
IN THE GRANT ERA

Reconstruction dramatically altered the South's political culture, at least for a time. Most of the state governments established under the radical plan were controlled by the Republicans. This was made possible by federal troops who guarded the polls, preventing fraud and intimidation. The Republican voters, and the official they elected, were a mixed bag. The largest number of Republican voters were blacks who naturally cast their ballots for the party of Lincoln without any urging. Some were native Southern whites—"scalawags"—who saw Republicanism as the wave of the future and sought to ride that wave. A few were "carpetbaggers," Northerners who had come South, primarily seeking economic opportunity, and became active in politics. Though blacks were the majority of the electorate, they were not the majority of the Republican officials. Still, many state legislators were former slaves and fourteen blacks, including two senators from Mississippi, were sent to Congress to represent former Confederate states.

Conservative whites charged these Radical administrations with corruption, extravagance, ignorance, and indifference. Critics described scenes of drunkenness on the capitol floors, of legislators betting public money at the race track, of lobbyists buying and selling politicians in full view of reporters.

But in fact the Radical governments in the South were no more corrupt than other local governments, and compared to some they were positively angelic. Don't forget that this was the era of Tammany Hall in New

York where a ring of crooked politicians was getting kickbacks from city contractors who grossly overcharged taxpayers, the time of the Whiskey Ring in St. Louis which was cheating the federal government of millions in taxes, and a time when the legislature in Harrisburg, Pennsylvania adjourned only when the Pennsylvania Railroad had no further favors to ask of its members. Moreover, the Radical governments had a long list of praiseworthy accomplishments. They established the first state funded public schools in the South; they helped rebuild the section's deteriorated railroads, public buildings, and levees; they modernized the state judicial systems; they created industrial commissions to attract Northern capital. But they were costly by conventional Southern standards and—here's what really bugged the Southern democrats—they treated blacks as equals. Conservative whites could not tolerate this, and worked hard to expel them. In every Republican controlled state in the South, conservative whites mounted aggressive campaigns to drive the Radicals from power and replace them with Democrats.

Their task was made easier because Radicalism was on the wane in both the North and the South. By the early 1870s many Northern defenders of black equality were becoming discouraged. No matter how much the federal government tried, it could not make white Southerners accept a truly color blind society. And whites, more numerous even in Dixie, and certainly richer and better educated than blacks, had the staying power to prevail. Short of extended military rule, how could those with the weaker hand be protected against those who had all the high cards? It was hopeless. "The truth is," declaimed a Republican politician in 1875, "our people are tired out with this worn out cry of 'Southern outrages!!!'."

And the war and the "everlasting Negro question"

THE KU KLUX KLAN

The Ku Klux Klan was a secret organization formed in 1866 by former Confederate officers as a fraternal order. The Klan quickly became a defender of white supremacy. Hooded Klansmen attacked blacks who complained of low wages or acted insolent; they whipped Yankees who taught in freedmen's schools; they burned black schoolhouses and murdered Republican leaders, black and white. The brutal process cut sharply into Republican strength in the South and helped redeem several states for conservative white rule. When state militias could not suppress the Klan, Congress intervened and made it a federal crime to interfere with any

person's political or civil rights. By the mid-1870s the original Klan had ceased its midnight rides, cross-burnings, and hooded demonstrations, though other klansmen soon took up the white supremacy cause.

Two early Klansmen in an illustration from Harper's Weekly, *December 10, 1868.*

had come to serve as a continuing excuse for widespread corrupt rule in Washington. Hiding behind the "bloody shirt" and the need to defend the freedmen, Republican politicians were able to rob the country blind. Under Grant, the country's moral tone sharply deteriorated. Every day seemed to reveal a new scandal involving administration officials or some prominent Republican. The president himself lacked a strong moral sense, and allowed his relatives to take advantage of his official position while he personally accepted favors from rich businessmen.

THE ELECTION OF 1872: THE NEWS-PAPER EDITOR VS. THE GENERAL

In 1872 a revolt within the Republican ranks led to the Liberal Republican movement dedicated to rescuing the nation from Grantism and the Democrats alike. The Liberal Republicans favored free trade, civil service reform, sound money, and reconciliation with the South. By some twist of fate they nominated the bewhiskered, cherubic Horace Greeley, the venerable and quixotic editor of the *New York Tribune,* as their presidential candidate in 1872. Greeley, peculiarly, also won the Democratic nomination, but in the end lost to Grant. Still, the Liberal Republican movement betokened a weakening resolve among Northerners to prop up the Radical state regimes in the South, and by 1876 only three Southern states, South Carolina, Louisiana, and Florida, were still governed by Republicans.

THE END OF RECONSTRUCTION

Rutherford B. Hayes (1822–1893). The Republican who became president in the disputed election of 1876.

In 1876, the Democrats nominated Samuel J. Tilden, as their presidential candidate. Their platform attacked Republican corruption and the rapacities of carpetbag tyrannies. The Republicans chose the former governor of Ohio, Rutherford Hayes, a man with a squeaky clean political record and a moderate view of the South. Their platform pushed for both permanent pacification of the South and exact equality in the exercise of all civil, political, and public rights—incompatible goals at this point.

TILDEN VS. HAYES: THE DISPUTED ELECTION OF 1876

On election day Tilden carried the Northern states of New York, Indiana, New Jersey, and Connecticut. The others went Republican. But what about the South? To beat Tilden, the Republicans would have to carry some of the former slave states. The returns made clear that Tilden had won all of the "redeemed" South, but in South Carolina, Florida, and Louisiana, where Republican administrations still clung to office, two conflicting sets of returns were being reported. If the Republican returns were valid, Hayes was president; if the Democratic, Tilden. As the public watched with dismay the nation began a four-month crisis of a disputed election.

In fact there had been fraud and intimidation on both sides and to this day there is no way to determine who would have won in a fair and square election. Congress tried to resolve the issue peaceably by establishing a fifteen-member electoral commission composed equally of representatives, senators, and Supreme Court judges. The initial appointees included seven Democrats and seven Republicans with one judge, David Davis, an independent. When Davis was unexpectedly elected to the Senate from Illinois his replacement from the Supreme Court was perforce a Republican, since there were no other Democratic justices left.

The commission's decision, issued piecemeal between February 9 and 28, favored the Republicans in each case by strict party vote of 8 to 7. Many Democrats, including Tilden, accepted defeat as inevitable and reconciled themselves to four more years of Republican rule. But Democratic firebrands threatened violence if their hero was cheated of election. Editor Henry Watterson of the *Louisville Courier-Journal* called for a march on Washington of 100,000 Democrats to protest the decision. In the

House of Representatives Democratic members threatened to filibuster the commission report until after Inauguration day thereby throwing the election of the president into the House of Representatives.

In the end, the voices of compromise prevailed. In behind-the-scenes negotiations, Southern Democrats and the Hayes people agreed that in exchange for a promise to accept the electoral commission decision, the Republican administration would pursue a policy of reconciliation toward the South. President Hayes would order federal troops out of the South thereby turning the last Republican states over to the Democrat redeemers. At the same time, to accommodate the wishes of Southern businessmen and entrepreneurs, Hayes promised to look with favor on southern calls for federal aid for railroads and other pork-barrel internal improvements legislation.

On March 5, 1877 Hayes peacefully took the oath of office as president. In April he ordered the last federal troops out of South Carolina and Louisiana, and the Democratic shadow governments waiting in the wings took over. Reconstruction, by the usual measure, was over.

It would leave behind a mixed legacy. For white liberals and black Americans it would seem a brief shining moment when a truly equal society appeared possible. It would inspire a Second Reconstruction eighty years later. To social conservatives it was a cautionary tale of misplaced philanthropy when the powerful central authority, ignoring racial realities and local wishes, attempted to change people's minds and behavior with bayonets. Few Americans today accept the second view, but whichever opinion is valid, by its end Reconstruction had created the "solid" Democratic South, a disenfranchised and economically stagnant black peasantry, and a section that increasingly would lose touch with the forces of "progress."